C-1316 CAREER EXAMINATION SERIES

This is your
PASSBOOK for...

Information Specialist

Test Preparation Study Guide
Questions & Answers

NATIONAL LEARNING CORPORATION®

COPYRIGHT NOTICE

This book is SOLELY intended for, is sold ONLY to, and its use is RESTRICTED to individual, bona fide applicants or candidates who qualify by virtue of having seriously filed applications for appropriate license, certificate, professional and/or promotional advancement, higher school matriculation, scholarship, or other legitimate requirements of education and/or governmental authorities.

This book is NOT intended for use, class instruction, tutoring, training, duplication, copying, reprinting, excerption, or adaptation, etc., by:

1) Other publishers
2) Proprietors and/or Instructors of "Coaching" and/or Preparatory Courses
3) Personnel and/or Training Divisions of commercial, industrial, and governmental organizations
4) Schools, colleges, or universities and/or their departments and staffs, including teachers and other personnel
5) Testing Agencies or Bureaus
6) Study groups which seek by the purchase of a single volume to copy and/or duplicate and/or adapt this material for use by the group as a whole without having purchased individual volumes for each of the members of the group
7) Et al.

Such persons would be in violation of appropriate Federal and State statutes.

PROVISION OF LICENSING AGREEMENTS – Recognized educational, commercial, industrial, and governmental institutions and organizations, and others legitimately engaged in educational pursuits, including training, testing, and measurement activities, may address request for a licensing agreement to the copyright owners, who will determine whether, and under what conditions, including fees and charges, the materials in this book may be used them. In other words, a licensing facility exists for the legitimate use of the material in this book on other than an individual basis. However, it is asseverated and affirmed here that the material in this book CANNOT be used without the receipt of the express permission of such a licensing agreement from the Publishers. Inquiries re licensing should be addressed to the company, attention rights and permissions department.

All rights reserved, including the right of reproduction in whole or in part, in any form or by any means, electronic or mechanical, including photocopying, recording, or by any information storage and retrieval system, without permission in writing from the Publisher.

Copyright © 2024 by
National Learning Corporation

212 Michael Drive, Syosset, NY 11791
(516) 921-8888 • www.passbooks.com
E-mail: info@passbooks.com

PUBLISHED IN THE UNITED STATES OF AMERICA

PASSBOOK® SERIES

THE *PASSBOOK® SERIES* has been created to prepare applicants and candidates for the ultimate academic battlefield – the examination room.

At some time in our lives, each and every one of us may be required to take an examination – for validation, matriculation, admission, qualification, registration, certification, or licensure.

Based on the assumption that every applicant or candidate has met the basic formal educational standards, has taken the required number of courses, and read the necessary texts, the *PASSBOOK® SERIES* furnishes the one special preparation which may assure passing with confidence, instead of failing with insecurity. Examination questions – together with answers – are furnished as the basic vehicle for study so that the mysteries of the examination and its compounding difficulties may be eliminated or diminished by a sure method.

This book is meant to help you pass your examination provided that you qualify and are serious in your objective.

The entire field is reviewed through the huge store of content information which is succinctly presented through a provocative and challenging approach – the question-and-answer method.

A climate of success is established by furnishing the correct answers at the end of each test.

You soon learn to recognize types of questions, forms of questions, and patterns of questioning. You may even begin to anticipate expected outcomes.

You perceive that many questions are repeated or adapted so that you can gain acute insights, which may enable you to score many sure points.

You learn how to confront new questions, or types of questions, and to attack them confidently and work out the correct answers.

You note objectives and emphases, and recognize pitfalls and dangers, so that you may make positive educational adjustments.

Moreover, you are kept fully informed in relation to new concepts, methods, practices, and directions in the field.

You discover that you are actually taking the examination all the time: you are preparing for the examination by "taking" an examination, not by reading extraneous and/or supererogatory textbooks.

In short, this PASSBOOK®, used directedly, should be an important factor in helping you to pass your test.

INFORMATION SPECIALIST

DUTIES
Under direct supervision, prepares public relations material for a department or agency and the work is carefully reviewed for completeness and accuracy. Related duties may also be performed, as required.

SUBJECT OF EXAMINATION
The written test will be designed to test for knowledge, skills, and/or abilities in such areas as:
1. Assuring copy reflects standard english practices;
2. Reviewing and editing copy;
3. Preparing written material; and
4. Educating and interacting with the public.

HOW TO TAKE A TEST

I. YOU MUST PASS AN EXAMINATION

A. WHAT EVERY CANDIDATE SHOULD KNOW

Examination applicants often ask us for help in preparing for the written test. What can I study in advance? What kinds of questions will be asked? How will the test be given? How will the papers be graded?

As an applicant for a civil service examination, you may be wondering about some of these things. Our purpose here is to suggest effective methods of advance study and to describe civil service examinations.

Your chances for success on this examination can be increased if you know how to prepare. Those "pre-examination jitters" can be reduced if you know what to expect. You can even experience an adventure in good citizenship if you know why civil service exams are given.

B. WHY ARE CIVIL SERVICE EXAMINATIONS GIVEN?

Civil service examinations are important to you in two ways. As a citizen, you want public jobs filled by employees who know how to do their work. As a job seeker, you want a fair chance to compete for that job on an equal footing with other candidates. The best-known means of accomplishing this two-fold goal is the competitive examination.

Exams are widely publicized throughout the nation. They may be administered for jobs in federal, state, city, municipal, town or village governments or agencies.

Any citizen may apply, with some limitations, such as the age or residence of applicants. Your experience and education may be reviewed to see whether you meet the requirements for the particular examination. When these requirements exist, they are reasonable and applied consistently to all applicants. Thus, a competitive examination may cause you some uneasiness now, but it is your privilege and safeguard.

C. HOW ARE CIVIL SERVICE EXAMS DEVELOPED?

Examinations are carefully written by trained technicians who are specialists in the field known as "psychological measurement," in consultation with recognized authorities in the field of work that the test will cover. These experts recommend the subject matter areas or skills to be tested; only those knowledges or skills important to your success on the job are included. The most reliable books and source materials available are used as references. Together, the experts and technicians judge the difficulty level of the questions.

Test technicians know how to phrase questions so that the problem is clearly stated. Their ethics do not permit "trick" or "catch" questions. Questions may have been tried out on sample groups, or subjected to statistical analysis, to determine their usefulness.

Written tests are often used in combination with performance tests, ratings of training and experience, and oral interviews. All of these measures combine to form the best-known means of finding the right person for the right job.

II. HOW TO PASS THE WRITTEN TEST

A. NATURE OF THE EXAMINATION

To prepare intelligently for civil service examinations, you should know how they differ from school examinations you have taken. In school you were assigned certain definite pages to read or subjects to cover. The examination questions were quite detailed and usually emphasized memory. Civil service exams, on the other hand, try to discover your present ability to perform the duties of a position, plus your potentiality to learn these duties. In other words, a civil service exam attempts to predict how successful you will be. Questions cover such a broad area that they cannot be as minute and detailed as school exam questions.

In the public service similar kinds of work, or positions, are grouped together in one "class." This process is known as *position-classification*. All the positions in a class are paid according to the salary range for that class. One class title covers all of these positions, and they are all tested by the same examination.

B. FOUR BASIC STEPS

1) Study the announcement

How, then, can you know what subjects to study? Our best answer is: "Learn as much as possible about the class of positions for which you've applied." The exam will test the knowledge, skills and abilities needed to do the work.

Your most valuable source of information about the position you want is the official exam announcement. This announcement lists the training and experience qualifications. Check these standards and apply only if you come reasonably close to meeting them.

The brief description of the position in the examination announcement offers some clues to the subjects which will be tested. Think about the job itself. Review the duties in your mind. Can you perform them, or are there some in which you are rusty? Fill in the blank spots in your preparation.

Many jurisdictions preview the written test in the exam announcement by including a section called "Knowledge and Abilities Required," "Scope of the Examination," or some similar heading. Here you will find out specifically what fields will be tested.

2) Review your own background

Once you learn in general what the position is all about, and what you need to know to do the work, ask yourself which subjects you already know fairly well and which need improvement. You may wonder whether to concentrate on improving your strong areas or on building some background in your fields of weakness. When the announcement has specified "some knowledge" or "considerable knowledge," or has used adjectives like "beginning principles of..." or "advanced ... methods," you can get a clue as to the number and difficulty of questions to be asked in any given field. More questions, and hence broader coverage, would be included for those subjects which are more important in the work. Now weigh your strengths and weaknesses against the job requirements and prepare accordingly.

3) Determine the level of the position

Another way to tell how intensively you should prepare is to understand the level of the job for which you are applying. Is it the entering level? In other words, is this the position in which beginners in a field of work are hired? Or is it an intermediate or advanced level? Sometimes this is indicated by such words as "Junior" or "Senior" in the class title. Other jurisdictions use Roman numerals to designate the level – Clerk I, Clerk II, for example. The word "Supervisor" sometimes appears in the title. If the level is not indicated by the title, check the description of duties. Will you be working under very close supervision, or will you have responsibility for independent decisions in this work?

4) Choose appropriate study materials

Now that you know the subjects to be examined and the relative amount of each subject to be covered, you can choose suitable study materials. For beginning level jobs, or even advanced ones, if you have a pronounced weakness in some aspect of your training, read a modern, standard textbook in that field. Be sure it is up to date and has general coverage. Such books are normally available at your library, and the librarian will be glad to help you locate one. For entry-level positions, questions of appropriate difficulty are chosen – neither highly advanced questions, nor those too simple. Such questions require careful thought but not advanced training.

If the position for which you are applying is technical or advanced, you will read more advanced, specialized material. If you are already familiar with the basic principles of your field, elementary textbooks would waste your time. Concentrate on advanced textbooks and technical periodicals. Think through the concepts and review difficult problems in your field.

These are all general sources. You can get more ideas on your own initiative, following these leads. For example, training manuals and publications of the government agency which employs workers in your field can be useful, particularly for technical and professional positions. A letter or visit to the government department involved may result in more specific study suggestions, and certainly will provide you with a more definite idea of the exact nature of the position you are seeking.

III. KINDS OF TESTS

Tests are used for purposes other than measuring knowledge and ability to perform specified duties. For some positions, it is equally important to test ability to make adjustments to new situations or to profit from training. In others, basic mental abilities not dependent on information are essential. Questions which test these things may not appear as pertinent to the duties of the position as those which test for knowledge and information. Yet they are often highly important parts of a fair examination. For very general questions, it is almost impossible to help you direct your study efforts. What we can do is to point out some of the more common of these general abilities needed in public service positions and describe some typical questions.

1) General information

Broad, general information has been found useful for predicting job success in some kinds of work. This is tested in a variety of ways, from vocabulary lists to questions about current events. Basic background in some field of work, such as sociology or economics, may be sampled in a group of questions. Often these are principles which have become familiar to most persons through exposure rather than through formal training. It is difficult to advise you how to study for these questions; being alert to the world around you is our best suggestion.

2) Verbal ability

An example of an ability needed in many positions is verbal or language ability. Verbal ability is, in brief, the ability to use and understand words. Vocabulary and grammar tests are typical measures of this ability. Reading comprehension or paragraph interpretation questions are common in many kinds of civil service tests. You are given a paragraph of written material and asked to find its central meaning.

3) Numerical ability
Number skills can be tested by the familiar arithmetic problem, by checking paired lists of numbers to see which are alike and which are different, or by interpreting charts and graphs. In the latter test, a graph may be printed in the test booklet which you are asked to use as the basis for answering questions.

4) Observation
A popular test for law-enforcement positions is the observation test. A picture is shown to you for several minutes, then taken away. Questions about the picture test your ability to observe both details and larger elements.

5) Following directions
In many positions in the public service, the employee must be able to carry out written instructions dependably and accurately. You may be given a chart with several columns, each column listing a variety of information. The questions require you to carry out directions involving the information given in the chart.

6) Skills and aptitudes
Performance tests effectively measure some manual skills and aptitudes. When the skill is one in which you are trained, such as typing or shorthand, you can practice. These tests are often very much like those given in business school or high school courses. For many of the other skills and aptitudes, however, no short-time preparation can be made. Skills and abilities natural to you or that you have developed throughout your lifetime are being tested.

Many of the general questions just described provide all the data needed to answer the questions and ask you to use your reasoning ability to find the answers. Your best preparation for these tests, as well as for tests of facts and ideas, is to be at your physical and mental best. You, no doubt, have your own methods of getting into an exam-taking mood and keeping "in shape." The next section lists some ideas on this subject.

IV. KINDS OF QUESTIONS

Only rarely is the "essay" question, which you answer in narrative form, used in civil service tests. Civil service tests are usually of the short-answer type. Full instructions for answering these questions will be given to you at the examination. But in case this is your first experience with short-answer questions and separate answer sheets, here is what you need to know:

1) **Multiple-choice Questions**
Most popular of the short-answer questions is the "multiple choice" or "best answer" question. It can be used, for example, to test for factual knowledge, ability to solve problems or judgment in meeting situations found at work.
A multiple-choice question is normally one of three types—
- It can begin with an incomplete statement followed by several possible endings. You are to find the one ending which *best* completes the statement, although some of the others may not be entirely wrong.
- It can also be a complete statement in the form of a question which is answered by choosing one of the statements listed.

- It can be in the form of a problem – again you select the best answer.

Here is an example of a multiple-choice question with a discussion which should give you some clues as to the method for choosing the right answer:

When an employee has a complaint about his assignment, the action which will *best* help him overcome his difficulty is to
- A. discuss his difficulty with his coworkers
- B. take the problem to the head of the organization
- C. take the problem to the person who gave him the assignment
- D. say nothing to anyone about his complaint

In answering this question, you should study each of the choices to find which is best. Consider choice "A" – Certainly an employee may discuss his complaint with fellow employees, but no change or improvement can result, and the complaint remains unresolved. Choice "B" is a poor choice since the head of the organization probably does not know what assignment you have been given, and taking your problem to him is known as "going over the head" of the supervisor. The supervisor, or person who made the assignment, is the person who can clarify it or correct any injustice. Choice "C" is, therefore, correct. To say nothing, as in choice "D," is unwise. Supervisors have and interest in knowing the problems employees are facing, and the employee is seeking a solution to his problem.

2) True/False Questions

The "true/false" or "right/wrong" form of question is sometimes used. Here a complete statement is given. Your job is to decide whether the statement is right or wrong.

SAMPLE: A roaming cell-phone call to a nearby city costs less than a non-roaming call to a distant city.

This statement is wrong, or false, since roaming calls are more expensive.

This is not a complete list of all possible question forms, although most of the others are variations of these common types. You will always get complete directions for answering questions. Be sure you understand *how* to mark your answers – ask questions until you do.

V. RECORDING YOUR ANSWERS

Computer terminals are used more and more today for many different kinds of exams.
For an examination with very few applicants, you may be told to record your answers in the test booklet itself. Separate answer sheets are much more common. If this separate answer sheet is to be scored by machine – and this is often the case – it is highly important that you mark your answers correctly in order to get credit.
An electronic scoring machine is often used in civil service offices because of the speed with which papers can be scored. Machine-scored answer sheets must be marked with a pencil, which will be given to you. This pencil has a high graphite content which responds to the electronic scoring machine. As a matter of fact, stray dots may register as answers, so do not let your pencil rest on the answer sheet while you are pondering the correct answer. Also, if your pencil lead breaks or is otherwise defective, ask for another.

Since the answer sheet will be dropped in a slot in the scoring machine, be careful not to bend the corners or get the paper crumpled.

The answer sheet normally has five vertical columns of numbers, with 30 numbers to a column. These numbers correspond to the question numbers in your test booklet. After each number, going across the page are four or five pairs of dotted lines. These short dotted lines have small letters or numbers above them. The first two pairs may also have a "T" or "F" above the letters. This indicates that the first two pairs only are to be used if the questions are of the true-false type. If the questions are multiple choice, disregard the "T" and "F" and pay attention only to the small letters or numbers.

Answer your questions in the manner of the sample that follows:

32. The largest city in the United States is
    A. Washington, D.C.
    B. New York City
    C. Chicago
    D. Detroit
    E. San Francisco

1) Choose the answer you think is best. (New York City is the largest, so "B" is correct.)
2) Find the row of dotted lines numbered the same as the question you are answering. (Find row number 32)
3) Find the pair of dotted lines corresponding to the answer. (Find the pair of lines under the mark "B.")
4) Make a solid black mark between the dotted lines.

VI. BEFORE THE TEST

Common sense will help you find procedures to follow to get ready for an examination. Too many of us, however, overlook these sensible measures. Indeed, nervousness and fatigue have been found to be the most serious reasons why applicants fail to do their best on civil service tests. Here is a list of reminders:

- Begin your preparation early – Don't wait until the last minute to go scurrying around for books and materials or to find out what the position is all about.
- Prepare continuously – An hour a night for a week is better than an all-night cram session. This has been definitely established. What is more, a night a week for a month will return better dividends than crowding your study into a shorter period of time.
- Locate the place of the exam – You have been sent a notice telling you when and where to report for the examination. If the location is in a different town or otherwise unfamiliar to you, it would be well to inquire the best route and learn something about the building.
- Relax the night before the test – Allow your mind to rest. Do not study at all that night. Plan some mild recreation or diversion; then go to bed early and get a good night's sleep.
- Get up early enough to make a leisurely trip to the place for the test – This way unforeseen events, traffic snarls, unfamiliar buildings, etc. will not upset you.
- Dress comfortably – A written test is not a fashion show. You will be known by number and not by name, so wear something comfortable.

- Leave excess paraphernalia at home – Shopping bags and odd bundles will get in your way. You need bring only the items mentioned in the official notice you received; usually everything you need is provided. Do not bring reference books to the exam. They will only confuse those last minutes and be taken away from you when in the test room.
- Arrive somewhat ahead of time – If because of transportation schedules you must get there very early, bring a newspaper or magazine to take your mind off yourself while waiting.
- Locate the examination room – When you have found the proper room, you will be directed to the seat or part of the room where you will sit. Sometimes you are given a sheet of instructions to read while you are waiting. Do not fill out any forms until you are told to do so; just read them and be prepared.
- Relax and prepare to listen to the instructions
- If you have any physical problem that may keep you from doing your best, be sure to tell the test administrator. If you are sick or in poor health, you really cannot do your best on the exam. You can come back and take the test some other time.

VII. AT THE TEST

The day of the test is here and you have the test booklet in your hand. The temptation to get going is very strong. Caution! There is more to success than knowing the right answers. You must know how to identify your papers and understand variations in the type of short-answer question used in this particular examination. Follow these suggestions for maximum results from your efforts:

1) Cooperate with the monitor

The test administrator has a duty to create a situation in which you can be as much at ease as possible. He will give instructions, tell you when to begin, check to see that you are marking your answer sheet correctly, and so on. He is not there to guard you, although he will see that your competitors do not take unfair advantage. He wants to help you do your best.

2) Listen to all instructions

Don't jump the gun! Wait until you understand all directions. In most civil service tests you get more time than you need to answer the questions. So don't be in a hurry. Read each word of instructions until you clearly understand the meaning. Study the examples, listen to all announcements and follow directions. Ask questions if you do not understand what to do.

3) Identify your papers

Civil service exams are usually identified by number only. You will be assigned a number; you must not put your name on your test papers. Be sure to copy your number correctly. Since more than one exam may be given, copy your exact examination title.

4) Plan your time

Unless you are told that a test is a "speed" or "rate of work" test, speed itself is usually not important. Time enough to answer all the questions will be provided, but this does not mean that you have all day. An overall time limit has been set. Divide the total time (in minutes) by the number of questions to determine the approximate time you have for each question.

5) Do not linger over difficult questions

If you come across a difficult question, mark it with a paper clip (useful to have along) and come back to it when you have been through the booklet. One caution if you do this – be sure to skip a number on your answer sheet as well. Check often to be sure that you have not lost your place and that you are marking in the row numbered the same as the question you are answering.

6) Read the questions

Be sure you know what the question asks! Many capable people are unsuccessful because they failed to *read* the questions correctly.

7) Answer all questions

Unless you have been instructed that a penalty will be deducted for incorrect answers, it is better to guess than to omit a question.

8) Speed tests

It is often better NOT to guess on speed tests. It has been found that on timed tests people are tempted to spend the last few seconds before time is called in marking answers at random – without even reading them – in the hope of picking up a few extra points. To discourage this practice, the instructions may warn you that your score will be "corrected" for guessing. That is, a penalty will be applied. The incorrect answers will be deducted from the correct ones, or some other penalty formula will be used.

9) Review your answers

If you finish before time is called, go back to the questions you guessed or omitted to give them further thought. Review other answers if you have time.

10) Return your test materials

If you are ready to leave before others have finished or time is called, take ALL your materials to the monitor and leave quietly. Never take any test material with you. The monitor can discover whose papers are not complete, and taking a test booklet may be grounds for disqualification.

VIII. EXAMINATION TECHNIQUES

1) Read the general instructions carefully. These are usually printed on the first page of the exam booklet. As a rule, these instructions refer to the timing of the examination; the fact that you should not start work until the signal and must stop work at a signal, etc. If there are any *special* instructions, such as a choice of questions to be answered, make sure that you note this instruction carefully.

2) When you are ready to start work on the examination, that is as soon as the signal has been given, read the instructions to each question booklet, underline any key words or phrases, such as *least, best, outline, describe* and the like. In this way you will tend to answer as requested rather than discover on reviewing your paper that you *listed without describing*, that you selected the *worst* choice rather than the *best* choice, etc.

3) If the examination is of the objective or multiple-choice type – that is, each question will also give a series of possible answers: A, B, C or D, and you are called upon to select the best answer and write the letter next to that answer on your answer paper – it is advisable to start answering each question in turn. There may be anywhere from 50 to 100 such questions in the three or four hours allotted and you can see how much time would be taken if you read through all the questions before beginning to answer any. Furthermore, if you come across a question or group of questions which you know would be difficult to answer, it would undoubtedly affect your handling of all the other questions.

4) If the examination is of the essay type and contains but a few questions, it is a moot point as to whether you should read all the questions before starting to answer any one. Of course, if you are given a choice – say five out of seven and the like – then it is essential to read all the questions so you can eliminate the two that are most difficult. If, however, you are asked to answer all the questions, there may be danger in trying to answer the easiest one first because you may find that you will spend too much time on it. The best technique is to answer the first question, then proceed to the second, etc.

5) Time your answers. Before the exam begins, write down the time it started, then add the time allowed for the examination and write down the time it must be completed, then divide the time available somewhat as follows:
    - If 3-1/2 hours are allowed, that would be 210 minutes. If you have 80 objective-type questions, that would be an average of 2-1/2 minutes per question. Allow yourself no more than 2 minutes per question, or a total of 160 minutes, which will permit about 50 minutes to review.
    - If for the time allotment of 210 minutes there are 7 essay questions to answer, that would average about 30 minutes a question. Give yourself only 25 minutes per question so that you have about 35 minutes to review.

6) The most important instruction is to *read each question* and make sure you know what is wanted. The second most important instruction is to *time yourself properly* so that you answer every question. The third most important instruction is to *answer every question*. Guess if you have to but include something for each question. Remember that you will receive no credit for a blank and will probably receive some credit if you write something in answer to an essay question. If you guess a letter – say "B" for a multiple-choice question – you may have guessed right. If you leave a blank as an answer to a multiple-choice question, the examiners may respect your feelings but it will not add a point to your score. Some exams may penalize you for wrong answers, so in such cases *only*, you may not want to guess unless you have some basis for your answer.

7) Suggestions
   a. Objective-type questions
      1. Examine the question booklet for proper sequence of pages and questions
      2. Read all instructions carefully
      3. Skip any question which seems too difficult; return to it after all other questions have been answered
      4. Apportion your time properly; do not spend too much time on any single question or group of questions

5. Note and underline key words – *all, most, fewest, least, best, worst, same, opposite,* etc.
6. Pay particular attention to negatives
7. Note unusual option, e.g., unduly long, short, complex, different or similar in content to the body of the question
8. Observe the use of "hedging" words – *probably, may, most likely,* etc.
9. Make sure that your answer is put next to the same number as the question
10. Do not second-guess unless you have good reason to believe the second answer is definitely more correct
11. Cross out original answer if you decide another answer is more accurate; do not erase until you are ready to hand your paper in
12. Answer all questions; guess unless instructed otherwise
13. Leave time for review

b. Essay questions
1. Read each question carefully
2. Determine exactly what is wanted. Underline key words or phrases.
3. Decide on outline or paragraph answer
4. Include many different points and elements unless asked to develop any one or two points or elements
5. Show impartiality by giving pros and cons unless directed to select one side only
6. Make and write down any assumptions you find necessary to answer the questions
7. Watch your English, grammar, punctuation and choice of words
8. Time your answers; don't crowd material

8) Answering the essay question

Most essay questions can be answered by framing the specific response around several key words or ideas. Here are a few such key words or ideas:

M's: manpower, materials, methods, money, management
P's: purpose, program, policy, plan, procedure, practice, problems, pitfalls, personnel, public relations

a. Six basic steps in handling problems:
1. Preliminary plan and background development
2. Collect information, data and facts
3. Analyze and interpret information, data and facts
4. Analyze and develop solutions as well as make recommendations
5. Prepare report and sell recommendations
6. Install recommendations and follow up effectiveness

b. Pitfalls to avoid
1. *Taking things for granted* – A statement of the situation does not necessarily imply that each of the elements is necessarily true; for example, a complaint may be invalid and biased so that all that can be taken for granted is that a complaint has been registered

2. *Considering only one side of a situation* – Wherever possible, indicate several alternatives and then point out the reasons you selected the best one
3. *Failing to indicate follow up* – Whenever your answer indicates action on your part, make certain that you will take proper follow-up action to see how successful your recommendations, procedures or actions turn out to be
4. *Taking too long in answering any single question* – Remember to time your answers properly

IX. AFTER THE TEST

Scoring procedures differ in detail among civil service jurisdictions although the general principles are the same. Whether the papers are hand-scored or graded by machine we have described, they are nearly always graded by number. That is, the person who marks the paper knows only the number – never the name – of the applicant. Not until all the papers have been graded will they be matched with names. If other tests, such as training and experience or oral interview ratings have been given, scores will be combined. Different parts of the examination usually have different weights. For example, the written test might count 60 percent of the final grade, and a rating of training and experience 40 percent. In many jurisdictions, veterans will have a certain number of points added to their grades.

After the final grade has been determined, the names are placed in grade order and an eligible list is established. There are various methods for resolving ties between those who get the same final grade – probably the most common is to place first the name of the person whose application was received first. Job offers are made from the eligible list in the order the names appear on it. You will be notified of your grade and your rank as soon as all these computations have been made. This will be done as rapidly as possible.

People who are found to meet the requirements in the announcement are called "eligibles." Their names are put on a list of eligible candidates. An eligible's chances of getting a job depend on how high he stands on this list and how fast agencies are filling jobs from the list.

When a job is to be filled from a list of eligibles, the agency asks for the names of people on the list of eligibles for that job. When the civil service commission receives this request, it sends to the agency the names of the three people highest on this list. Or, if the job to be filled has specialized requirements, the office sends the agency the names of the top three persons who meet these requirements from the general list.

The appointing officer makes a choice from among the three people whose names were sent to him. If the selected person accepts the appointment, the names of the others are put back on the list to be considered for future openings.

That is the rule in hiring from all kinds of eligible lists, whether they are for typist, carpenter, chemist, or something else. For every vacancy, the appointing officer has his choice of any one of the top three eligibles on the list. This explains why the person whose name is on top of the list sometimes does not get an appointment when some of the persons lower on the list do. If the appointing officer chooses the second or third eligible, the No. 1 eligible does not get a job at once, but stays on the list until he is appointed or the list is terminated.

X. HOW TO PASS THE INTERVIEW TEST

The examination for which you applied requires an oral interview test. You have already taken the written test and you are now being called for the interview test – the final part of the formal examination.

You may think that it is not possible to prepare for an interview test and that there are no procedures to follow during an interview. Our purpose is to point out some things you can do in advance that will help you and some good rules to follow and pitfalls to avoid while you are being interviewed.

What is an interview supposed to test?

The written examination is designed to test the technical knowledge and competence of the candidate; the oral is designed to evaluate intangible qualities, not readily measured otherwise, and to establish a list showing the relative fitness of each candidate – as measured against his competitors – for the position sought. Scoring is not on the basis of "right" and "wrong," but on a sliding scale of values ranging from "not passable" to "outstanding." As a matter of fact, it is possible to achieve a relatively low score without a single "incorrect" answer because of evident weakness in the qualities being measured.

Occasionally, an examination may consist entirely of an oral test – either an individual or a group oral. In such cases, information is sought concerning the technical knowledges and abilities of the candidate, since there has been no written examination for this purpose. More commonly, however, an oral test is used to supplement a written examination.

Who conducts interviews?

The composition of oral boards varies among different jurisdictions. In nearly all, a representative of the personnel department serves as chairman. One of the members of the board may be a representative of the department in which the candidate would work. In some cases, "outside experts" are used, and, frequently, a businessman or some other representative of the general public is asked to serve. Labor and management or other special groups may be represented. The aim is to secure the services of experts in the appropriate field.

However the board is composed, it is a good idea (and not at all improper or unethical) to ascertain in advance of the interview who the members are and what groups they represent. When you are introduced to them, you will have some idea of their backgrounds and interests, and at least you will not stutter and stammer over their names.

What should be done before the interview?

While knowledge about the board members is useful and takes some of the surprise element out of the interview, there is other preparation which is more substantive. It *is* possible to prepare for an oral interview – in several ways:

1) Keep a copy of your application and review it carefully before the interview

This may be the only document before the oral board, and the starting point of the interview. Know what education and experience you have listed there, and the sequence and dates of all of it. Sometimes the board will ask you to review the highlights of your experience for them; you should not have to hem and haw doing it.

2) Study the class specification and the examination announcement

Usually, the oral board has one or both of these to guide them. The qualities, characteristics or knowledges required by the position sought are stated in these documents. They offer valuable clues as to the nature of the oral interview. For example, if the job involves supervisory responsibilities, the announcement will usually indicate that knowledge of modern supervisory methods and the qualifications of the candidate as a supervisor will be tested. If so, you can expect such questions, frequently in the form of a hypothetical situation which you are expected to solve. NEVER go into an oral without knowledge of the duties and responsibilities of the job you seek.

3) Think through each qualification required

Try to visualize the kind of questions you would ask if you were a board member. How well could you answer them? Try especially to appraise your own knowledge and background in each area, *measured against the job sought*, and identify any areas in which you are weak. Be critical and realistic – do not flatter yourself.

4) Do some general reading in areas in which you feel you may be weak

For example, if the job involves supervision and your past experience has NOT, some general reading in supervisory methods and practices, particularly in the field of human relations, might be useful. Do NOT study agency procedures or detailed manuals. The oral board will be testing your understanding and capacity, not your memory.

5) Get a good night's sleep and watch your general health and mental attitude

You will want a clear head at the interview. Take care of a cold or any other minor ailment, and of course, no hangovers.

What should be done on the day of the interview?

Now comes the day of the interview itself. Give yourself plenty of time to get there. Plan to arrive somewhat ahead of the scheduled time, particularly if your appointment is in the fore part of the day. If a previous candidate fails to appear, the board might be ready for you a bit early. By early afternoon an oral board is almost invariably behind schedule if there are many candidates, and you may have to wait. Take along a book or magazine to read, or your application to review, but leave any extraneous material in the waiting room when you go in for your interview. In any event, relax and compose yourself.

The matter of dress is important. The board is forming impressions about you – from your experience, your manners, your attitude, and your appearance. Give your personal appearance careful attention. Dress your best, but not your flashiest. Choose conservative, appropriate clothing, and be sure it is immaculate. This is a business interview, and your appearance should indicate that you regard it as such. Besides, being well groomed and properly dressed will help boost your confidence.

Sooner or later, someone will call your name and escort you into the interview room. *This is it.* From here on you are on your own. It is too late for any more preparation. But remember, you asked for this opportunity to prove your fitness, and you are here because your request was granted.

What happens when you go in?

The usual sequence of events will be as follows: The clerk (who is often the board stenographer) will introduce you to the chairman of the oral board, who will introduce you to the other members of the board. Acknowledge the introductions before you sit down. Do not be surprised if you find a microphone facing you or a stenotypist sitting by. Oral interviews are usually recorded in the event of an appeal or other review.

Usually the chairman of the board will open the interview by reviewing the highlights of your education and work experience from your application – primarily for the benefit of the other members of the board, as well as to get the material into the record. Do not interrupt or comment unless there is an error or significant misinterpretation; if that is the case, do not hesitate. But do not quibble about insignificant matters. Also, he will usually ask you some question about your education, experience or your present job – partly to get you to start talking and to establish the interviewing "rapport." He may start the actual questioning, or turn it over to one of the other members. Frequently, each member undertakes the questioning on a particular area, one in which he is perhaps most competent, so you can expect each member to participate in the examination. Because time is limited, you may also expect some rather abrupt switches in the direction the questioning takes, so do not be upset by it. Normally, a board member will not pursue a single line of questioning unless he discovers a particular strength or weakness.

After each member has participated, the chairman will usually ask whether any member has any further questions, then will ask you if you have anything you wish to add. Unless you are expecting this question, it may floor you. Worse, it may start you off on an extended, extemporaneous speech. The board is not usually seeking more information. The question is principally to offer you a last opportunity to present further qualifications or to indicate that you have nothing to add. So, if you feel that a significant qualification or characteristic has been overlooked, it is proper to point it out in a sentence or so. Do not compliment the board on the thoroughness of their examination – they have been sketchy, and you know it. If you wish, merely say, "No thank you, I have nothing further to add." This is a point where you can "talk yourself out" of a good impression or fail to present an important bit of information. Remember, *you close the interview yourself*.

The chairman will then say, "That is all, Mr. _____, thank you." Do not be startled; the interview is over, and quicker than you think. Thank him, gather your belongings and take your leave. Save your sigh of relief for the other side of the door.

How to put your best foot forward

Throughout this entire process, you may feel that the board individually and collectively is trying to pierce your defenses, seek out your hidden weaknesses and embarrass and confuse you. Actually, this is not true. They are obliged to make an appraisal of your qualifications for the job you are seeking, and they want to see you in your best light. Remember, they must interview all candidates and a non-cooperative candidate may become a failure in spite of their best efforts to bring out his qualifications. Here are 15 suggestions that will help you:

1) Be natural – Keep your attitude confident, not cocky

If you are not confident that you can do the job, do not expect the board to be. Do not apologize for your weaknesses, try to bring out your strong points. The board is interested in a positive, not negative, presentation. Cockiness will antagonize any board member and make him wonder if you are covering up a weakness by a false show of strength.

2) Get comfortable, but don't lounge or sprawl

Sit erectly but not stiffly. A careless posture may lead the board to conclude that you are careless in other things, or at least that you are not impressed by the importance of the occasion. Either conclusion is natural, even if incorrect. Do not fuss with your clothing, a pencil or an ashtray. Your hands may occasionally be useful to emphasize a point; do not let them become a point of distraction.

3) Do not wisecrack or make small talk

This is a serious situation, and your attitude should show that you consider it as such. Further, the time of the board is limited – they do not want to waste it, and neither should you.

4) Do not exaggerate your experience or abilities
In the first place, from information in the application or other interviews and sources, the board may know more about you than you think. Secondly, you probably will not get away with it. An experienced board is rather adept at spotting such a situation, so do not take the chance.

5) If you know a board member, do not make a point of it, yet do not hide it
Certainly you are not fooling him, and probably not the other members of the board. Do not try to take advantage of your acquaintanceship – it will probably do you little good.

6) Do not dominate the interview
Let the board do that. They will give you the clues – do not assume that you have to do all the talking. Realize that the board has a number of questions to ask you, and do not try to take up all the interview time by showing off your extensive knowledge of the answer to the first one.

7) Be attentive
You only have 20 minutes or so, and you should keep your attention at its sharpest throughout. When a member is addressing a problem or question to you, give him your undivided attention. Address your reply principally to him, but do not exclude the other board members.

8) Do not interrupt
A board member may be stating a problem for you to analyze. He will ask you a question when the time comes. Let him state the problem, and wait for the question.

9) Make sure you understand the question
Do not try to answer until you are sure what the question is. If it is not clear, restate it in your own words or ask the board member to clarify it for you. However, do not haggle about minor elements.

10) Reply promptly but not hastily
A common entry on oral board rating sheets is "candidate responded readily," or "candidate hesitated in replies." Respond as promptly and quickly as you can, but do not jump to a hasty, ill-considered answer.

11) Do not be peremptory in your answers
A brief answer is proper – but do not fire your answer back. That is a losing game from your point of view. The board member can probably ask questions much faster than you can answer them.

12) Do not try to create the answer you think the board member wants
He is interested in what kind of mind you have and how it works – not in playing games. Furthermore, he can usually spot this practice and will actually grade you down on it.

13) Do not switch sides in your reply merely to agree with a board member
Frequently, a member will take a contrary position merely to draw you out and to see if you are willing and able to defend your point of view. Do not start a debate, yet do not surrender a good position. If a position is worth taking, it is worth defending.

14) Do not be afraid to admit an error in judgment if you are shown to be wrong

The board knows that you are forced to reply without any opportunity for careful consideration. Your answer may be demonstrably wrong. If so, admit it and get on with the interview.

15) Do not dwell at length on your present job

The opening question may relate to your present assignment. Answer the question but do not go into an extended discussion. You are being examined for a *new* job, not your present one. As a matter of fact, try to phrase ALL your answers in terms of the job for which you are being examined.

Basis of Rating

Probably you will forget most of these "do's" and "don'ts" when you walk into the oral interview room. Even remembering them all will not ensure you a passing grade. Perhaps you did not have the qualifications in the first place. But remembering them will help you to put your best foot forward, without treading on the toes of the board members.

Rumor and popular opinion to the contrary notwithstanding, an oral board wants you to make the best appearance possible. They know you are under pressure – but they also want to see how you respond to it as a guide to what your reaction would be under the pressures of the job you seek. They will be influenced by the degree of poise you display, the personal traits you show and the manner in which you respond.

ABOUT THIS BOOK

This book contains tests divided into Examination Sections. Go through each test, answering every question in the margin. We have also attached a sample answer sheet at the back of the book that can be removed and used. At the end of each test look at the answer key and check your answers. On the ones you got wrong, look at the right answer choice and learn. Do not fill in the answers first. Do not memorize the questions and answers, but understand the answer and principles involved. On your test, the questions will likely be different from the samples. Questions are changed and new ones added. If you understand these past questions you should have success with any changes that arise. Tests may consist of several types of questions. We have additional books on each subject should more study be advisable or necessary for you. Finally, the more you study, the better prepared you will be. This book is intended to be the last thing you study before you walk into the examination room. Prior study of relevant texts is also recommended. NLC publishes some of these in our Fundamental Series. Knowledge and good sense are important factors in passing your exam. Good luck also helps. So now study this Passbook, absorb the material contained within and take that knowledge into the examination. Then do your best to pass that exam.

EXAMINATION SECTION

SAMPLE QUESTIONS

COMMUNICATING WITH THE PUBLIC

DIRECTIONS: Each question or incomplete statement is followed by several suggested answers or completions. Select the one that BEST answers the question or completes the statement. *PRINT THE LETTER OF THE CORRECT ANSWER IN THE SPACE AT THE RIGHT.*

1. If others are within hearing distance while you are taking a confidential phone message, the BEST way to verify that the message is correct is to
   A. read the message back to the caller
   B. ask the caller to call back later
   C. explain that you will call back
   D. ask the caller to repeat the message

   1.____

2. In order to complete a certain task, you need to ask a favor of a worker you don't know very well. The BEST way to do this would be to
   A. ask him briefly stating your reasons
   B. convince him it is for the good of the office
   C. tell him how greatly he can benefit if he does it
   D. offer to do something for him in return

   2.____

KEY (CORRECT ANSWERS)

1. The correct answer is D. If the caller repeats the message to you, the other people in the room will not hear what he is saying, and you will be able to check the facts in the message.

2. The correct answer is A. Be businesslike and to the point when you ask for a work-related favor from a fellow worker.

EXAMINATION SECTION
TEST 1

DIRECTIONS: Each question or incomplete statement is followed by several suggested answers or completions. Select the one that BEST answers the question or completes the statement. *PRINT THE LETTER OF THE CORRECT ANSWER IN THE SPACE AT THE RIGHT.*

1. A specialist is meeting with a panel of local community leaders to determine their perceptions about the effectiveness of a recent outreach program. The leaders seem unresponsive to the specialist's questions, looking at the floor or each other without directly answering the specialist's questions.
   One strategy that might work to elicit the desired information would be to
   A. try to discern the hidden meaning of their silence
   B. adopt a mildly confrontational tone and remind them of what's at stake in the community
   C. keep asking open-ended questions and wait patiently for responses
   D. tell them to come back when they're ready to tell you their opinions

   1.____

2. Each of the following statements about maintaining a community's attention is true, EXCEPT:
   A. The more challenging it is to pay attention to a message, the more likely it is that it will be attended to
   B. Listeners will be more motivated to pay attention if a speech is personally meaningful
   C. People will be more likely to attend if a speaker pauses to suggest natural transitions in a speech
   D. Listeners will attend to messages that stand out

   2.____

3. Each of the following is a key strategy to integrative bargaining among community members in conflict, EXCEPT
   A. focusing on positions, rather than interests
   B. separating the people from the problem
   C. aiming for an outcome based on an objectively identified standard
   D. using active listening skills, such as rephrasing and questioning

   3.____

4. Which of the following is NOT one of the major variables to take into account when considering a community needs assessment?
   A. State of program development   B. Resources available
   C. Demographics   D. Community attitudes

   4.____

5. Which of the following groups would probably be formed specifically for, or be involved in, the purpose of addressing a specific unmet community need?
   A. An existing consumer group
   B. A council of community representatives
   C. A committee
   D. An existing community organization

   5.____

6. If a public outreach campaign designed to mobilize a community fails, the MOST likely reason for this failure is that the campaign
   A. was not specific about what it wanted people to do
   B. was overly serious and did not appeal to people's sense of humor
   C. offered no incentive for the audience to make a change
   D. did not use language that appealed to the audience's emotions

7. Nationwide, the rate of involvement of elderly people in community-based programs demonstrates that they are
   A. under-served when compared to other age groups
   B. served at about the same rate as other age groups
   C. over-served when compared to other age groups
   D. hardly served at all

8. In projecting the likelihood of an education program's success, a domestic violence specialist identifies every single event that must occur to complete the project. The specialist then arranges these events in sequential order and allocates time requirements for each. Finally, the total time is calculated and a model showing all their events and timelines is charted.
   The specialist has used
   A. a PERT chart   B. a simulation
   C. a Markov model   D. the critical path method

9. When working with members of a predominantly African-American community, specialists from other cultural backgrounds should be aware that African-Americans tend to express thoughts and feelings through descriptions of
   A. physically tangible sensations   B. problems to be analyzed
   C. corresponding analogies   D. spiritual issues

10. Local nonprofessionals should be considered useful to a specialist who is looking to undertake a community outreach or educational initiative.
    Which of the following is LEAST likely to be a characteristic or role demonstrated by these community members?
    A. Undertaking support functions at the agency
    B. Serving as a communication channel between the agency and clients
    C. Encouraging greater agency acceptance and credibility within the community
    D. Helping the agency to accomplish meaningful change

11. In working with Native American groups or clients, it is important to recognize that the GREATEST health problem facing their communities today is
    A. domestic violence   B. depression and suicide
    C. alcoholism   D. tuberculosis

12. A specialist is facilitating a cooperative conflict resolution session between community members who have different opinions about what kinds of intervention services should be offered by the local adult protective services agency.
    Which of the following is NOT a guideline that should be followed in this process?
    A. Early in the negotiations, ask each party to name the issues on which they will positively not yield.
    B. Try to get the parties to view the issue from other points of view, beside the two or three conflicting ones.
    C. Have each side volunteer what it would be willing to do to resolve the conflict.
    D. At the end of the session, draw up a formal agreement with agreed-upon actions for both parties.

13. A specialist wants to evaluate the effectiveness of a local women's shelter. The shelter has suffered from lax participation, given the number of women who have been abused in the surrounding area. The specialist wants to speak with the women in the community who did not follow up on referrals to the shelter, and begins by visiting some of these women. After gaining the trust of these women, the specialist asks for the names of women they know who might be in need of help with a domestic violence situation.
    The specialist's approach in this case is _____ sampling.
    A. maximum variation   B. snowball
    C. convenience   D. typical case

14. When it comes to perceiving messages, people typically DON'T
    A. tend to simplify causal connections and sometimes even seek a single cause to explain what may be a highly complex effect
    B. tend to perceive messages independently of a categorical framework, especially if the message may be distorted by such an interpretation
    C. have a predisposition toward accepting any pattern that a speaker offers to explain seemingly unconnected facts
    D. tend to interpret things in the way they are viewed by their reference group

15. The elder members of Native American communities, regardless of kinship, are MOST commonly referred to as
    A. the ancients   B. father or mother
    C. grandfather or grandmother D. chiefs

16. Each of the following is typically an objective of community mobilization, EXCEPT:
    A. To convince existing community resources to alter their services or work together to address an unmet need
    B. To gather and distribute information to consumers and agencies about unmet needs

C. To publicize existing community resources and make them more accessible
D. To bring an unmet community need to public attention in order to achieve acceptance of and support for fulfilling the need

17. Research in community outreach shows that women often build friendships through shared positive feelings, whereas men often build friendships through
    A. metacommunication
    B. catharsis
    C. impression management
    D. shared activities

    17.____

18. Typically, the FIRST step in a community-needs assessment is to
    A. identify community's strengths
    B. explore the nature of the neighborhood
    C. get to know the area and its residents
    D. talk to people in the community

    18.____

19. Most public relations experts agree that _____ exposure(s) to a message is the minimum just to get the message noticed. If the aim of a public outreach campaign is action or a change in behavior, the agency budget must plan for more exposures.
    A. one
    B. two
    C. three
    D. four

    19.____

20. In the program development/community liaison model of community work and public outreach, the PRIMARY constituency is considered to be
    A. community representatives and the service agency board or administrators
    B. elected officials, social agencies, and interagency organizations
    C. marginalized or oppressed population groups in a city or region
    D. residents of a neighborhood, parish or rural county

    20.____

21. Social or interpersonal problems in many African-American communities have their roots in
    A. personality deficits
    B. unresolved family conflicts
    C. poor communication
    D. external stressors

    21.____

22. A public outreach campaign should
    I. focus on short-term, measurable goals, rather than ultimate outcomes
    II. try to alter entrenched attitudes within a short time, with powerfully worded messages
    III. proceed in steps or phases, each of which lays out a mechanism that leads to the desired effect
    IV. ignore causes that led to a problem, and instead focus on solutions

    The CORRECT answer is:
    A. I and II
    B. II and III
    C. III only
    D. I, II, III and IV

    22.____

23. Research findings indicate that in listing preferences for helping professional attributes, individuals from culturally diverse groups are MOST likely to consider _____ as more important than _____.
    A. personality similarity; either race/ethnic similarity or attitude similarity
    B. therapist experience; any kind of similarity
    C. race/ethnic similarity; attitude similarity
    D. attitude similarity; race/ethnic similarity

24. Each of the following is considered to be an objective of community organization EXCEPT
    A. effecting changes in the distribution of decision-making power
    B. helping people develop and strengthen the traits of self-direction and cooperation
    C. effecting and maintaining the balance between needs and resources in a community
    D. helping people deal with their problems by developing alternative behaviors

25. A specialist is helping the adult protective services agency to design a public outreach campaign. The topic to be addressed is complex, public understanding is low, and most professionals at the agency feel that having more complete information might change the opinions of community members. Which method of pre-campaign research is probably MOST appropriate?
    A. Deliberative polling
    B. Attitude scales
    C. Surveys or questionnaires
    D. Focus groups

KEY (CORRECT ANSWERS)

1.	C	11.	C
2.	A	12.	A
3.	A	13.	B
4.	C	14.	B
5.	C	15.	C
6.	A	16.	B
7.	A	17.	D
8.	D	18.	B
9.	C	19.	C
10.	A	20.	A

21.	D
22.	C
23.	D
24.	D
25.	A

TEST 2

DIRECTIONS: Each question or incomplete statement is followed by several suggested answers or completions. Select the one that BEST answers the question or completes the statement. *PRINT THE LETTER OF THE CORRECT ANSWER IN THE SPACE AT THE RIGHT.*

1. A specialist has been called in to resolve a dispute between two community leaders who have been arguing about the level of service needed within the community. The discussion has been going on for several hours when the specialist arrives, and both people seem to be upset.
   After calming the two down and getting each of them to agree on a statement of the problem, the specialist should ask each person to
   A. summarize his or her argument in three main points
   B. explain why he or she became so upset
   C. clearly state, in objective terms, the position of the other in a form that meets with the other's approval
   D. identify the best alternative outcome, other than their presumed ideal

2. In evaluating the impact of a public outreach campaign, the _____ model can be used early in the campaign to address first impressions.
   A. exposure or advertising
   B. expert interview
   C. impact monitoring or process
   D. experimental or quasi-experimental

3. When trying to motivate an older population to take action on a community problem, it is helpful to remember that older people
   A. are more self-reliant in their decision-making than other members of the same family
   B. often need more time to decide than younger people
   C. are more likely than younger people to view community problems self-referentially
   D. tend to take a pragmatic, rather than philosophical, view of life

4. The method of group or community decision-making that is normally MOST time-consuming is
   A. majority opinion   B. consensus
   C. expert opinion   D. authority rule

5. A local adult protective services agency has identified one of the goals of its recent public outreach campaign to be the mobilization of activists.
   The campaign should probably
   A. target neutral audiences
   B. home in on supporters
   C. stick to purely factual information
   D. try to persuade community fence-sitters

1.____

2.____

3.____

4.____

5.____

6. Research of Native American youths' perceptions of family concerns for their well-being has generally found that these youths
   A. have a high degree of uncertainty about their families' feelings toward them
   B. believe their families don't care about them
   C. believe that their mothers care a great deal about them, but their fathers don't
   D. believe their families care a great deal about them

7. A domestic violence specialist is developing a new outreach program for the local community. The specialist has defined the target problem, set program goals, and planned the actions that will take place as a result of the program. Most likely, the next step will be to
   A. evaluate the resources available to achieve program goals
   B. define and sequence the steps that will be taken to achieve program goals
   C. determine how the program will be evaluated
   D. decide how the program will operate

8. Elder: *I'm so glad to have someone to talk to, someone who really understands my problem.*
   Specialist: *It is nice to be able to talk to someone who will listen.*
   Elder: *That's for sure.*
   In the above exchange, what listening skill is evident in the underlined statement?
   A. Verbatim response
   B. Paraphrasing
   C. Advising
   D. Evaluation

9. Which of the following activities is involved in the specialist's task of mobilizing?
   A. Meeting individuals in the community with problems and assisting them in finding help
   B. Identifying unmet community needs
   C. Speaking out against an unjust policy or procedure
   D. Developing new services or linking presently available services to meet community needs

10. The preliminary research associated with a public outreach campaign should FIRST be aimed at determining
    A. the budget
    B. the message's ultimate audience
    C. what media to use
    D. the short-term behavioral goals of the campaign

11. A specialist in a low-income community wants to plan programs that will deal with the influence of unemployment on domestic disturbances. The specialist needs to know not only how many unemployed people are in the community now, but also how many people will be unemployed at any particular tie in the future, and how those numbers will vary given certain conditions.

Probably the BEST way to trace employment rates over time and within differing conditions is through the use of
- A. the critical path
- B. linear programming
- C. difference equations
- D. the Markov model

12. Generally, public outreach programs—whatever their stated goal—should
   I. create a sense of urgency about a problem
   II. decline to identify opponents of the issue or idea
   III. propose concrete, easily understandable solutions
   IV. urge a specific action

   The CORRECT answer is:
   A. I only   B. I, III and IV   C. II and III   D. I, II, III and IV

13. Which of the following methods of community needs assessment relies to the GREATEST degree on existing public records?
   - A. Social indicators
   - B. Field study
   - C. Rates under treatment
   - D. Key informant

14. During an interview with a Native American client, a specialist is careful to maintain close and nearly constant eye contact.
   The client is MOST likely to interpret this as a(n)
   - A. show of high concern
   - B. sign of disrespect
   - C. uncomfortable assumption of intimacy
   - D. attempt to intimidate

15. The BEST strategy for addressing an audience that is known to be captive, or even hostile, is to
   - A. refer to experiences in common
   - B. flatter the audience
   - C. joke about things in or near the audience
   - D. plead for fairness

16. Integrative conflict resolution is characterized by
   - A. an overriding concern to maximize joint outcomes
   - B. one side's interests opposing the other's
   - C. a fixed and limited amount of resources to be divided, so that the more one group gets, the less another gets
   - D. manipulation and withholding information as negotiation strategies

17. A specialist wants to learn how to interact with the members of a largely Latino community in a more culturally sensitive way.
   Which of the following is NOT a guideline for interacting with members of a Latino community?
   - A. Efforts to foster independence and self-reliance may be interpreted by many Latinos as a lack of concern for others.
   - B. Efforts to deal one-on-one with an adolescent client may serve to alienate the parents, especially the mother.

C. A nonverbal gesture, such as lowering the eyes, is interpreted by many Latinos as a sign of respect and deference to authority.
D. In much of Latino culture, the focus of control for problems tends to be much more external than internal.

18. Each of the following is a supporting assumption of community organization, EXCEPT:
    A. Democracy requires cooperative participation.
    B. In order for communities to change, it is necessary for each individual in the community to be willing to change.
    C. Communities often need help with organization and planning.
    D. Holistic approaches work better than fragmented or ad-hoc programs.

19. Helping professionals often have difficulty to bring community resources together to fulfill unmet community needs.
    Which of the following is NOT usually a reason for this?
    A. Some community groups resist assistance when it is offered.
    B. Few community groups make their needs known.
    C. Community resources frequently change the type of services they offer.
    D. Often, community resources prefer to work alone.

20. When dealing with groups or populations of elderly clients, specialists should be mindful that about _____ of the nation's elderly suffer from mental health problems.
    A. a tenth   B. a quarter   C. a third   D. half

21. In an African-American community, a specialist from another culture should recognize that church participation, for most African-Americans, is viewed as a
    A. method for maintaining control and communicating competency
    B. way of depersonalizing problems or troubles
    C. way to divert attention away from problems
    D. means of cathartic emotional release

22. Adult protective service programs supported by state statutes protect elderly people from abuse and neglect under the doctrine of
    A. parens patriae   B. habeas corpus
    C. in loco parentis   D. volenti non fit injuria

23. In terms of public outreach, which of the following statements about an audience is NOT generally true?
    A. The more heterogeneous the audience, the more necessary it will be to use specific examples and appeals to certain types of people.
    B. The smaller the audience, the more likely that its members will share assumptions and values.
    C. When the speaker does not know the status of an audience, it is best to assume that they are captive rather than voluntary.
    D. The larger an audience, the more formal a presentation is likely to be.

24. A specialist often spends time in the places frequented by community residents. She listens carefully to what residents seem most concerned about, and engages many in conversations, asking them how they see the problems in the community. During these conversations, she makes mental notes about whether the statements of the problems are the same things that are mentioned in their conversations. From these conversations, the worker determines what she thinks the unmet needs of the community are.
Which of the key issues in identifying unmet needs has the worker neglected to address?
    A. The different points of view regarding the issues, and whether there is any common ground
    B. Whether the stated problems and conversations with community residents reflect the same concerns
    C. How community residents define the issues
    D. What the residents talk about with one another in a community

25. Which of the following political styles should be used to promote an issue that could become controversial if it is perceived to involve major reforms?
    A. High-conflict, polarized
    B. High-conflict, consensual
    C. Moderate conflict, compromise-oriented
    D. Low-conflict, technical

KEY (CORRECT ANSWERS)

1.	C		11.	D
2.	A		12.	B
3.	B		13.	A
4.	B		14.	B
5.	B		15.	A
6.	D		16.	A
7.	A		17.	D
8.	B		18.	B
9.	D		19.	C
10.	B		20.	B

21. D
22. A
23. A
24. A
25. D

EXAMINATION SECTION
TEST 1

DIRECTIONS: Each question or incomplete statement is followed by several suggested answers or completions. Select the one that BEST answers the question or completes the statement. *PRINT THE LETTER OF THE CORRECT ANSWER IN THE SPACE AT THE RIGHT.*

1. When conducting a needs assessment for the purpose of education planning, an agency's FIRST step is to identify or provide
   A. a profile of population characteristics
   B. barriers to participation
   C. existing resources
   D. profiles of competing resources

   1.____

2. Research has demonstrated that of the following, the MOST effective medium for communicating with external publics is(are)
   A. video news releases   B. television
   C. radio   D. newspapers

   2.____

3. Basic ideas behind the effort to influence the attitudes and behaviors of a constituency include each of the following EXCEPT the idea that
   A. words, rather than actions or events, are most likely to motivate
   B. demands for action are a usual response
   C. self-interest usually figures heavily into public involvement
   D. the reliability of change programs is difficult to assess

   3.____

4. An agency representative is trying to craft a pithy message to constituents in order to encourage the use of agency program resources.
   Choosing an audience for such messages is easiest when the message
   A. is project- or behavior-based   B. is combined with other messages
   C. is abstract   D. has a broad appeal

   4.____

5. Of the following factors, the MOST important to the success of an agency's external education or communication programs is the
   A. amount of resources used to implement them
   B. public's prior experiences with the agency
   C. real value of the program to the public
   D. commitment of the internal audience

   5.____

6. A representative for a state agency is being interviewed by a reporter from a local news network. The representative is being asked to defend a program that is extremely unpopular in certain parts of the municipality.
   When a constituency is known to be opposed to a position, the MOST useful communication strategy is to present

   6.____

A. only the arguments that are consistent with constituents' views
B. only the agency's side of the issue
C. both sides of the argument as clearly as possible
D. both sides of the argument, omitting key information about the opposing position

7. The MOST significant barriers to effective agency community relations include
   I. widespread distrust of communication strategies
   II. the media's "watchdog" stance
   III. public apathy
   IV. statutory opposition

   The CORRECT answer is:
   A. I only   B. I and II   C. II and III   D. III and IV

8. In conducting an education program, many agencies use workshops and seminars in a classroom setting.
   Advantages of classroom-style teaching over other means of educating the public include each of the following, EXCEPT
   A. enabling an instructor to verify learning through testing and interaction with the target audience
   B. enabling hands-on practice and other participatory learning techniques
   C. ability to reach an unlimited number of participants in a given length of time
   D. ability to convey the latest, most up-to-date information

9. The _____ model of community relations is characterized by an attempt to persuade the public to adopt the agency's point of view.
   A. two-way symmetric   B. two-way asymmetric
   C. public information   D. press agency/publicity

10. Important elements of an internal situation analysis include the
    I. list of agency opponents   II. communication audit
    III. updated organizational almanac   IV. stakeholder analysis

    The CORRECT answer is:
    A. I and II   B. I, II, and III   C. II and III   D. I, II, III and IV

11. Government agency information efforts typically involve each of the following objectives, EXCEPT to
    A. implement changes in the policies of government agencies to align with public opinion
    B. communicate the work of agencies
    C. explain agency techniques in a way that invites input from citizens
    D. provide citizen feedback to government administrators

12. Factors that are likely to influence the effectiveness of an educational campaign include the
    I. level of homogeneity among intended participants
    II. number and types of media used
    III. receptivity of the intended participants
    IV. level of specificity in the message or behavior to be taught

    The CORRECT answer is:
    A. I and II
    B. I, II, and III
    C. II and III
    D. I, II, III, and IV

13. An agency representative is writing instructional objectives that will later help to measure the effectiveness of an educational program.
    Which of the following verbs, included in an objective, would be MOST helpful for the purpose of measuring effectiveness?
    A. Know
    B. Identify
    C. Learn
    D. Comprehend

14. A state education agency wants to encourage participation in a program that has just received a boost through new federal legislation. The program is intended to include participants from a wide variety of socioeconomic and other demographic characteristics. The agency wants to launch a broad-based program that will inform virtually every interested party in the state about the program's new circumstances.
    In attempting to deliver this message to such a wide-ranging constituency, the agency's BEST practice would be to
    A. broadcast the same message through as many different media channels as possible
    B. focus on one discrete segment of the public at a time
    C. craft a message whose appeal is as broad as the public itself
    D. let the program's achievements speak for themselves and rely on word-of-mouth

15. Advantages associated with using the World Wide Web as an educational tool include
    I. an appeal to younger generations of the public
    II. visually-oriented, interactive learning
    III. learning that is not confined by space, time, or institutional association
    IV. a variety of methods for verifying use and learning

    The CORRECT answer is:
    A. I only
    B. I and II
    C. I, II, and III
    D. I, II, II, and IV

16. In agencies involved in health care, community relations is a critical function because it
    A. serves as an intermediary between the agency and consumers
    B. generates a clear mission statement for agency goals and priorities
    C. ensures patient privacy while satisfying the media's right to information
    D. helps marketing professionals determine the wants and needs of agency constituents

17. After an extensive campaign to promote its newest program to constituents, an agency learns that most of the audience did not understand the intended message.
MOST likely, the agency has
   A. chosen words that were intended to inform, rather than persuade
   B. not accurately interpreted what the audience really needed to know
   C. overestimated the ability of the audience to receive and process the message
   D. compensated for noise that may have interrupted the message

18. The necessary elements that lead to conviction and motivation in the minds of participants in an educational or information program include each of the following, EXCEPT the _____ of the message.
   A. acceptability   B. intensity
   C. single-channel appeal   D. pervasiveness

19. Printed materials are often at the core of educational programs provided by public agencies.
The PRIMARY disadvantage associated with print is that it
   A. does not enable comprehensive treatment of a topic
   B. is generally unreliable in term of assessing results
   C. is often the most expensive medium available
   D. is constrained by time

20. Traditional thinking on public opinion holds that there is about _____ percent of the public who are pivotal to shifting the balance and momentum of opinion—they are concerned about an issue, but not fanatical, and interested enough to pay attention to a reasoned discussion.
   A. 2   B. 10   C. 33   D. 51

21. One of the most useful guidelines for influencing attitude change among people is to
   A. invite the target audience to come to you, rather than approaching them
   B. use moral appeals as the primary approach
   C. use concrete images to enable people to see the results of behaviors or indifference
   D. offer tangible rewards to people for changes in behavior

22. An agency is attempting to evaluate the effectiveness of its educational program. For this purpose, it wants to observe several focus groups discussing the same program.
Which of the following would NOT be a guideline for the use of focus groups?
   A. Focus groups should only include those who have participated in the program.
   B. Be sure to accurately record the discussion.
   C. The same questions should be asked at each focus group meeting.
   D. It is often helpful to have a neutral, non-agency employee facilitate discussions.

23. Research consistently shows that _____ is the determinant most likely to make a newspaper editor run a news release.
    A. novelty   B. prominence   C. proximity   D. conflict

24. Which of the following is NOT one of the major variables to take into account when considering a population-needs assessment?
    A. State of program development   B. Resources available
    C. Demographics   D. Community attitudes

25. The FIRST step in any communications audit is to
    A. develop a research instrument
    B. determine how the organization currently communicates
    C. hire a contractor
    D. determine which audience to assess

KEY (CORRECT ANSWERS)

1.	A		11.	A
2.	D		12.	D
3.	A		13.	B
4.	A		14.	B
5.	D		15.	C
6.	C		16.	A
7.	D		17.	B
8.	C		18.	C
9.	B		19.	B
10.	C		20.	B

21. C
22. A
23. C
24. C
25. D

TEST 2

DIRECTIONS: Each question or incomplete statement is followed by several suggested answers or completions. Select the one that BEST answers the question or completes the statement. *PRINT THE LETTER OF THE CORRECT ANSWER IN THE SPACE AT THE RIGHT.*

1. A public relations practitioner at an agency has just composed a press release highlighting a program's recent accomplishments and success stories.
   In pitching such releases to print outlets, the practitioner should
   I. e-mail, mail, or send them by messenger
   II. address them to "editor" or "news director"
   III. have an assistant call all media contacts by telephone
   IV. ask reporters or editors how they prefer to receive them

   The CORRECT answer is:
   A. I and II   B. I and IV   C. II, III, and IV   D. III only

   1.____

2. The "output goals" of an educational program are MOST likely to include
   A. specified ratings of services by participants on a standardized scale
   B. observable effects on a given community or clientele
   C. the number of instructional hours provided
   D. the number of participants served

   2.____

3. An agency wants to evaluate satisfaction levels among program participants, and mails out questionnaires to everyone who has been enrolled in the last year.
   The PRIMARY problem associated with this method of evaluative research is that it
   A. poses a significant inconvenience for respondents
   B. is inordinately expensive
   C. does not allow for follow-up or clarification questions
   D. usually involves a low response rate

   3.____

4. A communications audit is an important tool for measuring
   A. the depth of penetration of a particular message or program
   B. the cost of the organization's information campaigns
   C. how key audiences perceive an organization
   D. the commitment of internal stakeholders

   4.____

5. The "ABCs" of written learning objectives include each of the following, EXCEPT
   A. Audience   B. Behavior   C. Conditions   D. Delineation

   5.____

6. When attempting to change the behaviors of constituents, it is important to keep in mind that
   I. most people are skeptical of communications that try to get them to change their behaviors
   II. in most cases, a person selects the media to which he exposes himself
   III. people tend to react defensively to messages or programs that rely on fear as a motivating factor
   IV. programs should aim for the broadest appeal possible in order to include as many participants as possible

   The CORRECT answer is:
   A. I and II   B. I, II and III   C. II and III   D. I, II, III, and IV

7. The "laws" of public opinion include the idea that it is
   A. useful for anticipating emergencies
   B. not sensitive to important events
   C. basically determined by self-interest
   D. sustainable through persistent appeals

8. Which of the following types of evaluations is used to measure public attitudes before and after an information/educational program?
   A. Retrieval study   B. Copy test
   C. Quota sampling   D. Benchmark study

9. The PRIMARY source for internal communications is(are) usually
   A. flow charts   B. meetings
   C. voice mail   D. printed publications

10. An agency representative is putting together informational materials—brochures and a newsletter—outlining changes in one of the state's biggest benefits programs.
    In assembling print materials as a medium for delivering information to the public, the representative should keep in mind each of the following trends:
    I. For various reasons, the reading capabilities of the public are in general decline
    II. Without tables and graphs to help illustrate the changes, it is unlikely that the message will be delivered effectively
    III. Professionals and career-oriented people are highly receptive to information written in the form of a journal article or empirical study
    IV. People tend to be put off by print materials that use itemized and bulleted (●) lists

    The CORRECT answer is:
    A. I and II   B. I, II and III   C. II and III   D. I, II, III, and IV

11. Which of the following steps in a problem-oriented information campaign would typically be implemented FIRST?
    A. Deciding on tactics
    B. Determining a communications strategy
    C. Evaluating the problem's impact
    D. Developing an organizational strategy

11._____

12. A common pitfall in conducting an educational program is to
    A. aim it at the wrong target audience
    B. overfund it
    C. leave it in the hands of people who are in the business of education, rather than those with expertise in the business of the organization
    D. ignore the possibility that some other organization is meeting the same educational need for the target audience

12._____

13. The key factors that affect the credibility of an agency's educational program include
    A. organization
    B. scope
    C. sophistication
    D. penetration

13._____

14. Research on public opinion consistently demonstrates that it is
    A. easy to move people toward a strong opinion on anything, as long as they are approached directly through their emotions
    B. easier to move people away from an opinion they currently hold than to have them form an opinion about something they have not previously cared about
    C. easy to move people toward a strong opinion on anything, as long as the message appeals to their reason and intellect
    D. difficult to move people toward a strong opinion on anything, no matter what the approach

14._____

15. In conducting an education program, many agencies use meetings and conferences to educate an audience about the organization and its programs. Advantages associated with this approach include
    I. a captive audience that is known to be interested in the topic
    II. ample opportunities for verifying learning
    III. cost-efficient meeting space
    IV. the ability to provide information on a wider variety of subjects

    The CORRECT answer is:
    A. I and II   B. I, III and IV   C. II and III   D. I, II, III and IV

15._____

16. An agency is attempting to evaluate the effectiveness of its educational programs. For this purpose, it wants to observe several focus groups discussing particular programs.
    For this purpose, a focus group should never number more than _____ participants.
    A. 5   B. 10   C. 15   D. 20

16._____

17. A _____ speech is written so that several agency members can deliver it to different audiences with only minor variations.
    A. basic   B. printed   C. quota   D. pattern

18. Which of the following statements about public opinion is generally considered to be FALSE?
    A. Opinion is primarily reactive rather than proactive.
    B. People have more opinions about goals than about the means by which to achieve them.
    C. Facts tend to shift opinion in the accepted direction when opinion is not solidly structured.
    D. Public opinion is based more on information than desire.

19. An agency is trying to promote its educational program.
    As a general rule, the agency should NOT assume that
    A. people will only participate if they perceive an individual benefit
    B. promotions need to be aimed at small, discrete groups
    C. if the program is good, the audience will find out about it
    D. a variety of methods, including advertising, special events, and direct mail, should be considered

20. In planning a successful educational program, probably the first and most important question for an agency to ask is:
    A. What will be the content of the program?
    B. Who will be served by the program?
    C. When is the best time to schedule the program?
    D. Why is the program necessary?

21. Media kits are LEAST likely to contain
    A. fact sheets   B. memoranda
    C. photographs with captions   D. news releases

22. The use of pamphlets and booklets as media for communication with the public often involves the disadvantage that
    A. the messages contained within them are frequently nonspecific
    B. it is difficult to measure their effectiveness in delivering the message
    C. there are few opportunities for people to refer to them
    D. color reproduction is poor

23. The MOST important prerequisite of a good educational program is an
    A. abundance of resources to implement it
    B. individual staff unit formed for the purpose of program delivery
    C. accurate needs assessment
    D. uneducated constituency

24. After an education program has been delivered, an agency conducts a program evaluation to determine whether its objectives have been met.
General rules about how to conduct such an education program valuation include each of the following, EXCEPT that it
   A. must be done immediately after the program has been implemented
   B. should be simple and easy to use
   C. should be designed so that tabulation of responses can take place quickly and inexpensively
   D. should solicit mostly subjective, open-ended responses if the audience was large

25. Using electronic media such as television as means of educating the public is typically recommended ONLY for agencies that
   I. have a fairly simple message to begin with
   II. want to reach the masses, rather than a targeted audience
   III. have substantial financial resources
   IV. accept that they will not be able to measure the results of the campaign with much precision

   The CORRECT answer is:
      A. I and II   B. I, II and III   C. II and IV   D. I, II, III and IV

KEY (CORRECT ANSWERS)

1.	B	11.	C
2.	C	12.	D
3.	D	13.	A
4.	C	14.	D
5.	D	15.	B
6.	B	16.	B
7.	C	17.	D
8.	D	18.	D
9.	D	19.	C
10.	A	20.	D

21.	B
22.	B
23.	C
24.	D
25.	D

EXAMINATION SECTION

TEST 1

DIRECTIONS: Each question or incomplete statement is followed by several suggested answers or completions. Select the one that BEST answers the question or completes the statement. *PRINT THE LETTER OF THE CORRECT ANSWER IN THE SPACE AT THE RIGHT.*

1. You are preparing a press release announcing a cornerstone laying ceremony for a housing project named after a prominent New Yorker. You desire to include in this press release some information about this person's contributions to public housing.
   Of the following sources which are available to you, the BEST one to go to in order to obtain verified information is
   A. the index and issues of a local newspaper obtainable in the public library
   B. Wikipedia
   C. a book on the history of public housing
   D. a biography of the individual

   1.____

2. You have been assigned to prepare a press release announcing the issuance of applications for apartments at a new city housing project.
   Of the following items of information, the one which is LEAST important to include in such a press release is the
   A. average building cost per apartment
   B. rental charges per room
   C. number of apartments in the project
   D. special facilities available at the project

   2.____

3. A company executive has asked you to assist him in preparing a presentation he is to deliver at a city board meeting concerning the potential benefits of a new government computer system. Members of the city administration will be present, as well as the press and the general public.
   Of the following, the theme you should emphasize MOST in this presentation is
   A. faster load times and stronger WiFi in all government buildings
   B. the inadequacies of the current computer system
   C. more efficient processing of city permits, payments and other transactions between the city and residents
   D. benefits of a digitally connected community

   3.____

4. You have been assigned to prepare a nightlife brochure that is to include photos of people dining at area restaurants. However, the photos you have are not adequate, so you run an image search on Google and find more suitable photos to use in the brochure.
   This practice is generally unacceptable because

   4.____

A. readers might notice that the people in the images are not actually dining at area restaurants
B. information on Google is not properly fact-checked
C. photos published on the internet cannot be used in print publications
D. use of the images might violate copyright law

5. It is your job to promote the fact that all pumpkins to be sold at an upcoming Fall Festival are harvested from local farms. Which of the following is the most effective way to ensure residents of the community are aware of this?
    A. Post notes on Twitter and Instagram, and tag the associated farms
    B. Run a print and online "Buy Local" campaign in the weeks leading up to the festival
    C. Publish a series of farmer profiles in the community newspaper
    D. Hang banners over local roads highlighting the festival and its amenities

6. Which of the following, about the opening of a new village dog park, is MOST appropriate according to standard rules of headline writing?
    A. YELPS OF DELIGHT YESTERDAY AS NEW DOG PARK OPENS TO CROWD OF 30 PUPS
    B. NEW FAIRMOUNT DOG PARK OFF TO "RUFF" START
    C. DOGGIE DESTINATION OPENED YESTERDAY IN FAIRMOUNT
    D. MORE BARK THAN BITE: DOG PARK OPENS IN FAIRMOUNT TO HOWLS OF GLORY FROM PUPS AND THEIR OWNERS

7. Suppose that you are assigned to release department information to reporters for the metropolitan press.
Of the following, the LEAST desirable practice for you to adopt in this assignment is
    A. as a general rule, release information in written form only
    B. set regular dates for the release of department news insofar as possible
    C. secure clearance for the issuance of all written releases
    D. release information first to reporters for newspapers which give the best coverage to department news

8. A letter from a private citizen, complaining about a department policy which has worked a hardship on him, has been referred to you for reply. The citizen asks that this policy be changed.
In answering this letter, it would be BEST to give major emphasis to
    A. an explanation of the reasons which make such a policy necessary
    B. pointing out that the department regulations cannot be revised to suit each individual case
    C. stating that the operations of any large organization must result in some hardships
    D. inducing the individual to come into the office where the matter can better be dealt with in a face-to-face interview

9. Suppose you are assigned to prepare the annual report for your department. Each bureau has been asked to submit a written report on its activities for the preceding year.
   Of the following, the MOST desirable action for you to take in carrying out this assignment is to
   A. return to the bureau heads for revision those reports which, in your opinion, contain unimportant material
   B. rewrite the material submitted by the bureaus to secure improved style without changing content
   C. arrange a conference with the bureau heads to discuss the reports they are to submit
   D. write an introduction and conclusion and let the reports of the bureaus constitute, unaltered, the body of the annual report

9._____

10. You have been assigned by your supervisor to do the preliminary editing of material written by other information assistants. After a week in this assignment, you evaluate the material submitted by one information assistant as of lower quality than that of the others.
    Of the following, the BEST action for you to take is to
    A. analyze his work with the other information assistants
    B. continue to edit his work without comment at this time
    C. suggest to him that he take a refresher course in writing
    D. recommend his transfer to less original work

10._____

11. You have completed gathering the necessary data for a routine newspaper release you are to write.
    The MOST desirable step for you to take next is to
    A. write a first draft of the release
    B. work out a plan for the release, including the beginning, the main points, and the ending
    C. develop a suitable title and then begin to write
    D. have someone familiar with the field check the accuracy of the data which you have gathered

11._____

12. Of the following writing techniques, the one which is generally LEAST effective for making written material more forceful is the
    A. repetition of a key word or phrase
    B. liberal use of exclamation points, capitalization, underlining and other similar devices
    C. use of the verbs in the active voice, rather than the passive voice
    D. use of a brief sentence, rather than a longer one, to express the same idea

12._____

13. The use of anecdotes and other verbal illustrations in writing is desirable PRIMARILY because
    A. this is a good way of showing the author's interest in his subject
    B. the reader will remember the anecdotes
    C. the illustrations will help the reader to remember the author's main idea
    D. the illustrations will entertain the reader

13._____

14. You are sending an e-mail to local community groups alerting them to a new youth sports program in municipal parks. It is considered good practice to include links to the department's social media accounts because
    A. it is an opportunity to gain more followers
    B. people respond more favorably to social media links
    C. sports programs are a popular topic on social media
    D. it provides additional outlets for readers to find detailed program information

15. The one of the following which is considered LEAST important in good news-writing is
    A. complete accuracy of names and addresses
    B. full identification of sources of information
    C. strict chronological order of presentation
    D. avoiding the use of editorial statements

16. Of the following, the BEST procedure to follow when writing an article to be read by experts is to
    A. avoid the technical terms as far as possible
    B. explain the technical terms the first time they are used
    C. use the technical terms of the experts
    D. use your literary judgment as to whether to use the technical terms

17. Of the following, the purpose for which it is LEAST important for a writer to have a large vocabulary is to
    A. give him a wider choice of synonyms and antonyms
    B. enable him to express himself in a sophisticated language
    C. improve his reading comprehension
    D. make his writing more exact

18. "The family lived in a small edifice on Maple Street."
    The preceding sentence involves a
    A. good choice of words
    B. poor choice of words because an "edifice" is large rather than small
    C. poor choice of words because the word "edifice" is obsolete
    D. poor choice of words because the word "edifice" is unfamiliar to the average reader

19. In fiction, the BEST way of acquainting the reader with the traits of the characters is through
    A. action
    B. dialogue and description
    C. action and dialogue
    D. dialogue

20. Subheads in an informal pamphlet
    A. are a matter of individual preference
    B. are appropriate only if the subject readily breaks itself down into separate sections
    C. should be used because the pamphlet will be easier to read
    D. should NOT be used because they look "textbookish"

21. The length of an average paragraph should
    A. be about 300 words
    B. harmonize with other elements of a writer's style
    C. not fall below 60 words
    D. vary according to each writing assignment

    21.____

22. In writing an informational blog post for young readers, it is advisable to include which of the following in order to hold readers' attention?
    A. Bulleted lists
    B. Links to relevant Twitter posts
    C. YouTube and TikTok videos
    D. All of the above

    22.____

23. Fictitious characters in factual writing should
    A. be disguised to make them appear real
    B. be given names rather than symbols
    C. be given symbols, such as A, B, and C, rather than names
    D. not be used

    23.____

24. "Clichés should be avoided in writing."
    The one of the following which is NOT a cliché is
    A. "every Tom, Dick and Harry"
    B. "left no stone unturned"
    C. "outrageous possibilities"
    D. "strike while the iron is hot"

    24.____

25. Public polling indicates that the majority of the American people are unacquainted with such items of general and historical information as the United Nations, the Enron scandal and the Y2K scare.
    Of the following, the MOST probable cause for this lack of knowledge is that
    A. people generally don't read enough to grasp this information
    B. most people don't know anything about current events or international relations
    C. schools avoid the teaching of controversial subjects
    D. this news was not dealt with in the newspapers read by the people polled

    25.____

26. The *Readers' Guide to Periodical Literature* is
    A. a digit of magazine articles
    B. a literary magazine
    C. an index of magazine articles
    D. an annual guide to magazines

    26.____

27. To publicize a senior citizens' golf outing hosted by the village parks department, you would likely reach the highest volume of interested participants by running a
    A. Facebook post targeted to seniors living in the state
    B. potentially viral TikTok video
    C. full-page ad in the village newspaper
    D. newspaper profile of the local golf pro

    27.____

28. All of the following are terms associated with publishing software EXCEPT
    A. point size
    B. click-through rate
    C. stock templates
    D. ePub

    28.____

29. Your department budget allocated $25,000 this year to be used specifically for digital marketing and promotion. Your supervisor has instructed you to use the money to update and modernize the department's web presence and increase reach. Of the following, the best use of these funds would be to
    A. set up a weekly podcast that features members of the community and how their work relates to the department
    B. improve SEO so that information about the department is more visible when community residents search for it
    C. hire a web designer to lay out a new website
    D. create an ongoing social media campaign that focuses on photos and short videos related to department functions and events in the community

30. The e-mail field used to send a press release to 50 local journalists is
    A. To   B. CC   C. Incognito   D. BCC

31. Of the following sentences, the one which is poorly written because it contains a "dangling construction" is:
    A. After waiting half an hour for the bus, I remembered that I had no money for carfare.
    B. Having returned from our vacations, the supervisor made reassignments.
    C. Smiling pleasantly, she acknowledged the applause of the audience.
    D. Walking over to him, I introduced myself and offered to help him catch his assailant.

Questions 32-36.

DIRECTIONS: Questions 32 through 36 consist of three sentences each. For each question, select the sentence which contains NO error in grammar or usage and write the capital letter preceding that sentence in the space at the right.

32. A. Be sure that everybody brings his notes to the conference.
    B. He looked like he meant to hit the boy.
    C. Mr. Jones is one of the clients who was chosen to represent the district.
    D. All are incorrect.

33. A. He is taller than I.
    B. I'll have nothing to do with these kind of people.
    C. The reason why he will not buy the house is because it is too expensive.
    D. All are incorrect.

34. A. Aren't I eligible for this apartment.
    B. Have you seen him anywheres?
    C. He should of come earlier.
    D. All are incorrect.

35. A. He graduated college in 1982.
    B. He hadn't but one more line to write.
    C. Who do you think is the author of this report?
    D. All are incorrect.

36. A. I talked to one official, whom I knew was fully impartial. 36.____
    B. Everyone signed the petition but him.
    C. He proved not only to be a good student but also a good athlete.
    D. All are incorrect.

Questions 37-40.

DIRECTIONS: Questions 37 through 40 consist of three sentences each. For each item, select the sentence which contains NO error in word usage and write the capital letter preceding that sentence in the space at the right.

37. A. Every year a large amount of tenants are admitted to housing projects. 37.____
    B. Henry Ford owned around a billion dollars in industrial equipment.
    C. He was aggravated by the child's bead behavior.
    D. All are incorrect.

38. A. Before he was committed to the asylum he suffered from the illusion that he was Napoleon. 38.____
    B. Besides stocks, there were also bonds in the safe.
    C. We bet the other team easily.
    D. All are incorrect.

39. A. Bring this report to your supervisor immediately. 39.____
    B. He set the chair down near the table.
    C. The capitol of New York is Albany.
    D. All are incorrect.

40. A. He was chosen to arbitrate the dispute because everyone knew he would be disinterested. 40.____
    B. It is advisable to obtain the best council before making an important decision,
    C. Less college students are interested in teaching than ever before.
    D. All are incorrect.

KEY (CORRECT ANSWERS)

1.	D	11.	B	21.	D	31.	B
2.	A	12.	B	22.	D	32.	A
3.	C	13.	C	23.	B	33.	A
4.	D	14.	D	24.	C	34.	D
5.	B	15.	C	25.	A	35.	C
6.	B	16.	C	26.	C	36.	B
7.	D	17.	B	27.	C	37.	D
8.	A	18.	B	28.	B	38.	B
9.	C	19.	C	29.	D	39.	B
10.	B	20.	C	30.	D	40.	A

TEST 2

DIRECTIONS: Each question or incomplete statement is followed by several suggested answers or completions. Select the one that BEST answers the question or completes the statement. *PRINT THE LETTER OF THE CORRECT ANSWER IN THE SPACE AT THE RIGHT.*

1. "Study your audience and slant your writing toward it."
   Of the following, the BEST procedure to adopt in applying this principle is to
   A. estimate the intelligence of your audience and write accordingly
   B. use the simplest possible prose style
   C. write about the things you believe your audience wants to read, rather than the things you would prefer to write about
   D. write about what you want to say in the form that is most likely to appeal to your audience

   1.____

2. "The first rule for giving your writing 'punch' is to take the most important idea and save it until the end of the sentence."
   Of the following sentences, the one which BEST illustrates this principle is:
   A. After they had notified the police, and had searched the entire neighborhood for hours, they found the little girl in the attic, sleeping peacefully.
   B. The enemy has destroyed the lives of our people, plundered our seas, ravaged our coasts, and burnt our towns.
   C. The thief had stolen the top-secret report, broken open the safe, and rifled the desk.
   D. The tornado left ruin and death in its wake and tore down every building in the village.

   2.____

3. "America has been built by the cooperative effort of many different kinds of people, working together."
   In the preceding sentence, a word or phrase which is NOT made superfluous by the use of another word or phrase of similar meaning is
   A. different   B. kinds of
   C. many   D. working together

   3.____

4. "The company did so well this year that, at the end of the year, it gave each employee a carton of cigarettes, a bottle of wine, and – a $100 bond."
   In the preceding sentence, the dash
   A. adds more force to the words which follow
   B. detracts from the force of the words which follow
   C. is an illustration of the improper use of punctuation
   D. neither adds nor detracts from the force of the words which follow

   4.____

5. An e-mail written by another information assistant begins with this sentence: "We beg to acknowledge your note sent to us on the 23rd." It then goes on to reply directly to the matters raised in the note of the 23rd.

   5.____

If you are assigned to edit this e-mail for clarity, the MOST desirable action of the following for you to take is to
- A. change the first sentence to read: "We beg to acknowledge your note sent to us on the 23rd and in reply wish to state that...."
- B. leave the first sentence as it is
- C. leave the first sentence unchanged but add another immediately following summarizing what the note of the 23rd inquired about
- D. omit the first sentence in its entirety

6. "Write as you talk" is an axiom widely accepted by news writers. Newspaper readers have a better chance of grasping the news if it is told to them simply and clearly.
The MOST direct implication of the preceding statement is that
- A. an axiom is a statement whose truth is generally accepted by everyone
- B. flowery readers are no different from newspaper reporters
- C. newspaper readers are no different from newspaper reporters
- D. the use of ungrammatical constructions is sometimes justified in writing for the newspapers

7. "Nowadays, lack of information usually goes hand in hand with little education; similarly, lack of information also usually goes hand in hand with low income. So, if you are writing for people in the lower income brackets or people who haven't gone to college, it's a good guess that they won't have much background knowledge."
The preceding statement implies MOST directly that
- A. little education has always been negatively correlated with little information
- B. poor people are usually not well-informed
- C. people who have not gone to college are in the lower income brackets
- D. writing for the poor and uneducated is more difficult than writing for the rich and well-educated

8. "Prices of building materials are, in the aggregate, more rigid than those of other commodities. Concentration of control over the supply of goods is frequently advanced as the explanation for price rigidities in general and for building materials in particular."
According to the preceding statement,
- A. increased demand and concurrent fixed supply are frequently responsible for increased prices of building materials
- B. in the aggregate, the high cost of building materials contributes substantially to the high cost of new housing construction
- C. the cost of most articles is generally more flexible than the cost of articles required in the construction of new buildings
- D. the existence of faulty methods of distribution is often advanced as an argument to explain price inequities

9. "In undertaking a new development, the builder first decides upon the price or rental range of the dwellings he proposes to construct. Then, after roughly estimating the cost of the selected structure, he tries to find land at suitable prices."
   According to the preceding statement,
   A. after a new development is completed, the builder adds up his construction and land costs and fixes the price of the individual house accordingly
   B. it is difficult to predict the probable cost of a new dwelling unit because of constant fluctuation in the cost of building materials
   C. land costs influence the selling price of dwellings least
   D. the selling price of a house is usually determined before construction is begun

9.____

10. "A construction program initiated by public agencies better protects the home buyer and insures the greater soundness of the neighborhood."
    According to the preceding statement,
    A. a home buyer is more confident of the safety of his investment if he is given to understand that the neighborhood will not change
    B. a public agency is more responsible in construction programs than a private builder could hope to be
    C. since a public agency can, if necessary, control the development of a neighborhood through zoning laws, public housing is more desirable
    D. to ensure the soundness of a neighborhood it is more effective to have the building of new homes planned by public agencies

10.____

11. "To achieve sound planning we cannot rely on educating the builder to the fact that what is good for the public will be ultimately good for him, for his interest is usually short term and the pattern in which he functions is not set up for voluntary reform."
    According to the preceding statement,
    A. a builder is not interested in educating the public to its ultimate benefits
    B. builders whose interests are usually of short duration can be educated to set up voluntary reforms
    C. since a builder's interest in any property is usually of short duration, he will voluntarily function for public benefit
    D. we cannot rely on educating a builder to the fact that public benefit is to his advantage in the long run

11.____

12. "If cities had a long-range objective, if they had plans showing the expected line of growth, plans for their future schools and parks, their houses and their locations, their industries and their locations, their future transportation facilities and their utilities, then with the advent of an emergency requiring government spending they could channel the expenditures and step up the program along the lines of the larger long-term plans."

12.____

According to the preceding statement,
- A. a city wishing to eliminate slums can with proper planning take advantage of an emergency requiring the channeling of expenditures
- B. an emergency requires the channeling of expenditures so that greater efficiency can be shown in planning
- C. cities which have long-range plans can make better use of the funds spent by the government during a depression
- D. long-range objectives help a city to devise new plans for the development of parks, schools, and other public improvements at a considerable saving

13. "Increment or decrement in city income hangs largely upon the maintenance of the values and valuations of real property, upon the quantity of new improvements that go into the city, upon the profitableness of real estate, upon the advent of booms and depressions, and upon the flow of people into or out of the city."
According to the preceding statement,
- A. a boom or a depression has a marked effect on the flow of people into or out of a city
- B. new improvements that go into a city enhance the profitableness of real estate
- C. real estate values, which form the major basis of a city's taxation, are the sources of city salaries
- D. the valuation of a city's income depends on the values of the real estate in the city

14. "The institution of the family is a vitally important part of all human societies, but in modern society, particularly, various organized services have developed that enable some people to secure some of the most essential benefits of family life without belonging to a family group."
Of the following, the LEAST valid inference on the basis of the preceding statement is that
- A. people who are not part of a family unit can obtain most of the essential benefits of family life by contacting an appropriate social agency
- B. present day society offers an opportunity to some who are not members of a family unit to share in some of the benefits of family living
- C. the institution of the family is not native to modern society alone
- D. to obtain the benefits of family life it is usually necessary to belong to a family group

15. "Reform organizations seek, as a rule, to bring about a specific economic or political change; social work agencies are usually occupied with the task of meeting existing situations in the lives of particular individuals or groups."
According to the preceding statement,
- A. a reform organization is concerned with helping the individual by changing some factor in the environment which the individual feels is too arduous to accept
- B. a reform organization is not concerned with the ability of the individual to meet his social responsibilities

C. social work agencies are not concerned with any specific economic or political change because this does not involve the individual's personal adjustment
D. social workers are primarily concerned with helping their clients to meet current living conditions

16. "Adequate facilities for education, recreation and health must be provided for children, and social conditions created that promote the child's development into law-abiding citizens. It is not the task of social work to provide these facilities but to direct children to them and to help them to use these facilities."
Of the following, the MOST accurate statement on the basis of the preceding statement is that
    A. A child who does not have adequate educational, recreational and health facilities will develop into a poor citizen
    B. the education of the public to the importance of providing adequate facilities for children is primarily the social worker's responsibility
    C. the proper use of leisure time by children is an important aspect of the social worker's job
    D. the three most important needs of a child which must be satisfied first are those of education, recreation and health

16.____

17. "Social workers start from the assumption that preservation of the family as the basic unit of social living is their accepted objective. In view of the frequency of divorce and the breakdown of authority in the home, social work now makes articulate its concern for family integrity."
According to the preceding statement,
    A. failure to keep the family as a basic unit leads to a breakdown of authority in the home, upsetting family integrity
    B. in extreme cases where divorce is inevitable a social worker must accept the breakdown of the family unit
    C. social workers are primarily concerned with keeping a family together as a basis entity of social living
    D. the importance of the family to society has been demonstrated by experience with children who have been institutionalized

17.____

18. "The marked change in the spirit in which social work is carried on is evidenced in the adoption of business methods of organization, including centralized purchasing of supplies for social agencies, cost accounting, careful budgeting and auditing of accounts, evaluation of methods and publication of reports. Trained personnel for defined jobs is increasingly sought, and there is appreciation of the differentiated abilities required in the social agency."
According to the preceding statement,
    A. it is apparent that the adoption of business methods of organization has resulted in a change in the method of preparing case work reports
    B. social work agencies that train people for definite jobs achieve savings in social work that approximate those of business organization

18.____

C. social work now uses current business procedures in carrying forward the purposes of a social agency
D. trained personnel in social work are responsible for the adoption of business methods of procedure

19. "Basic to the functioning of the professional social worker is an understanding of human personality and of the world we live in."
The one of the following which is the MOST accurate statement on the basis of the preceding quotation is that
    A. a social worker must be familiar with human behavior in order to be able to perform his work properly
    B. a social worker who understands human personality is able to function better as a citizen of the world
    C. social work may be classified as a profession because, for its proper performance, a basic understanding of the social and biological sciences is required
    D. through his daily contact with his clients a social worker will obtain a better understanding of the world he lives in

19.____

Questions 20-24.

DIRECTIONS: Questions 20 through 24 each consist of three words. For each item, select the word which is INCORRECTLY spelled and write the capital letter preceding that word in the space at the right.

20. A. achievment   B. maintenance   20.____
    C. questionnaire   D. all are correct

21. A. prevelant   B. pronunciation   21.____
    C. separate   D. all are correct

22. A. permissible   B. relevant   22.____
    C. seize   D. all are correct

23. A. corroborate   B. desparate   23.____
    C. eighth   D. all are correct

24. A. exceed   B. feasibility   24.____
    C. psycological   D. all are correct

Questions 25-29.

DIRECTIONS: Questions 25 through 29 are to be answered on the basis of the following information.

Copy I is an accurate copy of material which is to be prepared for the printer. Copy II of this material contains a number of typographical errors. Compare Copy II with Copy I and find the typographical errors. Every group of four lines in Copy II is numbered. Indicate the number of typographical errors in each group of lines of Copy II by writing in the correspondingly numbered space at the right the capital letter preceding the best of the following alternatives.

- A. No errors
- B. 1-2 errors
- C. 3-4 errors
- D. 5 or more errors

COPY I

Parcel 1. Beginning at a point formed by the intersection of the northerly side of 73rd avenue with the westerly side of Francis Lewis boulevard as said streets are indicated upon the final map of the borough of Queens known as Alteration Map No. 2831 adopted by the board of estimate on May 15, 1941; running thence northerly along the westerly side of Francis Lewis boulevard following a curve having a radius of 8,053 feet for a distance of 585.15 feet; thence northerly along the westerly side of Francis Lewis boulevard in a straight line for a distance of 687.43 feet; thence northerly along the westerly side of Francis Lewis boulevard and its prolongation following a curve having a radius of 5.667 feet for a distance of 509.79 feet to the old southerly side of North Hempstead turnpike as formerly laid out and as shown discontinued upon the aforementioned final city map; thence easterly along said southerly side of North Hempstead turnpike for 110.12 feet to the easterly side of Francis Lewis boulevard; thence southerly along the easterly side of Francis Lewis boulevard following a curve having a radius of 5.783 feet for a distance of 489.20 feet; thence southerly along the easterly side of Francis Lewis boulevard in a straight line for a distance of 687.43 feet; thence southerly along the easterly side of Francis Lewis boulevard following a curve having a radius of 7,947 feet for a distance of 572.90 feet to the northerly side of 73rd avenue.

COPY II

25. Parcel 1. Beginning at point formed by the intersection of the northerly side of 73rd Avenue with the westerly side of Francis Lewis boulevard as said streets are indicated upon the final map of the borough of Queens known as Alteration Map No. 2831 adapted by the board of estimate on May15, 1941; 25.____

26. running thence northerly along the westerly side of Francis Lewis boulevard following a curve having a radius of 8,053 feet for a distance of 585.15 feet; thence northerly along the westerly side of Francis Lewis boulevard in a straight line for a distance of 687.43 feet; thence northerly along 26.____

27. the westerly side of Francis Lewis boulevard and its prolongation following a curve having a radius of 5.677 feet for a distance of 509.79 feet to the old southerly side of North Hempstead Turnpike as formerly laid out and is shown discontinued upon the aforementioned final city map; thence easterly 27.____

28. along said southerly side of North Hempstead turnpike for 1101.2 feet to the easterly side of Francis Lewis boulevard; thence southerly along the easterly side of Francis Lewis boulevard following a curve having a radius of 5.783 feet for a distance of 489.20 feet; thence southerly along the easterly

28.____

29. side of Francis Lewis boulevard in a straight line for a distance of 687.43 feet; thence southerly along the easterly side of Francis Lewis boulevard following a curve having a radius of 7,947 feet for a distance of 572.09 feet to the northerly side of 73rd avenue.

29.____

30. "He described a hypothetical situation to illustrate his point."
In the preceding sentence, the word "hypothetical" means MOST NEARLY
    A. actual   B. theoretical   C. typical   D. unusual

30.____

31. "I gave tacit approval to my partner's proposed business changes."
In the preceding sentence, the word "tacit" means MOST NEARLY
    A. enthusiastic   B. partial   C. silent   D. written

31.____

32. "Jones was considered an astute lawyer by the members of his profession."
In the preceding sentence, the word "astute" means MOST NEARLY
    A. clever   B. persevering
    C. poorly trained   D. unethical

32.____

33. "There were intimations even in early days of the way in which he would go."
In the preceding sentence, the word "intimations" means MOST NEARLY
    A. hints   B. patterns   C. plans   D. purposes

33.____

34. "His last book was published posthumously."
In the preceding sentence, the word "posthumously" means MOST NEARLY
    A. after the death of the author   B. printed free by the publisher
    C. without a dedication   D. without royalties

34.____

35. "When he was challenged, he used every known subterfuge."
In the preceding sentence, the word "subterfuge" means MOST NEARLY
    A. evasion to justify one's conduct
    B. means of attack to defend one's self
    C. medical device
    D. unconscious thought

35.____

36. "His partner suggested a course of action that would alleviate the difficulties which confronted him."
In the preceding sentence, the word "alleviate" means MOST NEARLY
    A. correct   B. lessen   C. remove   D. solve

36.____

37. "Among the applicants for the new apartment white-collar workers were preponderant."
In the preceding sentence, the word "preponderant" means MOST NEARLY
    A. considered not eligible   B. in evidence
    C. superior in number   D. the first to apply

37.____

38. "The captain gave a lucid explanation of his plans for the coming campaign." 38.____
    In the preceding sentence, the word "lucid" means MOST NEARLY
    A. clear   B. graphic   C. interesting   D. thorough

39. "He led a sedentary life." 39.____
    In the preceding sentence, the word "sedentary" means MOST NEARLY
    A. aimless   B. exciting   C. full   D. inactive

40. "His plan for the next campaign was very plausible." 40.____
    In the preceding sentence, the word "plausible" means MOST NEARLY
    A. appropriate   B. believable   C. usable   D. valuable

KEY (CORRECT ANSWERS)

1.	D	11.	D	21.	A	31.	C
2.	A	12.	C	22.	D	32.	A
3.	C	13.	D	23.	B	33.	A
4.	A	14.	A	24.	C	34.	A
5.	D	15.	D	25.	C	35.	A
6.	B	16.	C	26.	A	36.	B
7.	B	17.	C	27.	C	37.	C
8.	C	18.	C	28.	B	38.	A
9.	D	19.	A	29.	B	39.	D
10.	D	20.	A	30.	B	40.	B

EXAMINATION SECTION
TEST 1

DIRECTIONS: Each question or incomplete statement is followed by several suggested answers or completions. Select the one that BEST answers the question or completes the statement. *PRINT THE LETTER OF THE CORRECT ANSWER IN THE SPACE AT THE RIGHT.*

1. The informed editorial assistant knows that the difference between a copy reader and a proofreader is that the copy reader
    A. checks copy against type proofs
    B. checks galleys
    C. edits material submitted by writers
    D. holds copy for the proofreader

    1.____

2. *Style* to a copy editor means
    A. following a set pattern when rules of spelling and punctuation are equivocal
    B. following the rules of formal grammar
    C. making sure that the writing is not elegant
    D. making sure that the writing is polished

    2.____

3. An unbound copy of a book that has yet to be proofread is often called a
    A. galley proof
    B. copy draft
    C. folio
    D. pre-proof

    3.____

4. A tool in word-processing software that allows multiple users to make and accept revisions is known as
    A. spell check
    B. track changes
    C. cell merge
    D. simple revise

    4.____

5. One of the proofreader's primary responsibilities is to ensure that
    A. a magazine feature follows house style guidelines
    B. news sources have been properly vetted
    C. an article uses proper punctuation
    D. a story is concise while including all pertinent information

    5.____

6. According to standard editing protocol, to abbreviate the word *Company*, as in Jones Widget Company, a copy editor should
    A. circle the word
    B. cross out excess letters and put a period over the *m*
    C. cross out the entire word and write *Co.* above it in the space between the lines
    D. cross out the entire word and write *Co.* in margin, running a line to its position

    6.____

41

7. In editing copy, it is often necessary to indicate that numerals are to be spelled out. This is done by
   A. circling the numeral
   B. crossing out the numeral and spelling it out between the lines
   C. crossing out the numeral and spelling it out in margin with a line drawn to its position
   D. drawing a square around the numeral

7.____

8. Multi-user software that allows writers, editors and other editorial personnel to collaborate on documents in real time is known as a
   A. content management system
   B. collaborative management system
   C. digital publishing portal
   D. desktop publishing application

8.____

9. Type size is measured
   A. ems   B. inches   C. picas   D. points

9.____

10. A pica measures approximately _____ and is typically used in _____.
    A. 1/6 of an inch; Microsoft Word
    B. 1/6 of an inch; Adobe InDesign
    C. 1/12 of an inch; Microsoft Excel
    D. 1/12 of an inch; QuarkXPress

10.____

11. Columns are measured in
    A. ems
    B. fractions of a page
    C. picas
    D. points

11.____

12. 36 points is
    A. about an inch
    B. about half an inch
    C. about two inches
    D. none of the foregoing

12.____

13. Which of the following is MOST relevant to news writers and editors?
    A. Chicago Manual of Style
    B. APA Publication Manual
    C. Associated Press Stylebook
    D. New York Times Manual of Style

13.____

14. The letters in italic type
    A. are less cursive than in roman type
    B. are more formal than in roman type
    C. are set by hand
    D. slant bottom left to top right

14.____

15. Sans-serif type
    A. has no additional fonts
    B. has no curlicues
    C. has no hangers or risers
    D. is old-fashioned German type

15.____

Questions 16-20.

DIRECTIONS: Questions 16 through 20 consist of groups of four words.
Select answer A if only ONE word is spelled correctly in a group.
Select answer B if TWO words are spelled correctly in a group,
Select answer C if THREE words are spelled correctly in a group.
Select answer D if all FOUR words are spelled correctly in a group.

16. counterfeit   embarass   panicky   supercede   16.____
17. benefited   personnel   questionnaire unparalelled   17.____
18. bankruptcy   describable proceed   vacuum   18.____
19. handicapped   mispell   offerred   pilgrimmage   19.____
20. corduroy   interfere   privilege   separator   20.____

Questions 21-25.

DIRECTIONS: For each question numbered 21 through 25, select the option whose meaning is MOST NEARLY the same as that of the numbered item.

21. CONDONE   21.____
    A. complete   B. condemn   C. cooperate   D. pardon

22. EXTENUATE   22.____
    A. accuse   B. excuse   C. lengthen   D. narrow

23. MORDANT   23.____
    A. caustic   B. depressed C. dying   D. unwholesome

24. SPATE   24.____
    A. broad road   B. excessive quantity
    C. fish eggs   D. mineral springs

25. TORTUOUS   25.____
    A. devious   B. foul   C. injurious   D. painful

KEY (CORRECT ANSWERS)

1.	C	11.	C
2.	A	12.	B
3.	A	13.	C
4.	B	14.	D
5.	C	15.	B
6.	A	16.	B
7.	A	17.	C
8.	A	18.	D
9.	D	19.	A
10.	B	20.	D

21. D
22. B
23. A
24. B
25. A

TEST 2

DIRECTIONS: Each question or incomplete statement is followed by several suggested answers or completions. Select the one that BEST answers the question or completes the statement. *PRINT THE LETTER OF THE CORRECT ANSWER IN THE SPACE AT THE RIGHT.*

1. Of the following, the one that is NOT a main responsibility of a magazine or newspaper writer is 1.____
   A. writing the article's headline
   B. choosing the quotes to run in the story
   C. interviewing sources with relevant information
   D. writing for the intended audience

2. Press releases received by a newspaper are usually directed to the 2.____
   A. city editor   B. managing editor
   C. promotion manager   D. publisher

3. The agency of the United States Government that supervises radio and television broadcasting is known by the abbreviation 3.____
   A. ABC   B. FCC   C. FTC   D. SEC

4. In a news article, the *nut graph* (or *graf*) is used 4.____
   A. to separate and highlight the most important quotes
   B. as a key visual element that enhances the story
   C. to detail the most pertinent information and why it is important
   D. to display the writer's contact information

5. Of the following, the type of publicity MOST likely to promote morale of the employees of your department would be a(n) 5.____
   A. article concerning the department written for a technical publication
   B. article in the annual report summarizing the activities of the department
   C. local newspaper article on the accomplishments of the employees of the agency
   D. short blurb on your superior carried by the Associated Press

6. If you wanted one photograph of a street accident to illustrate the need for improving traffic control at the scene of the accident, you should select a picture that shows 6.____
   A. a close-up of the cars and the victim
   B. a policeman questioning witnesses at the accident scene
   C. the cars and the victim against the whole intersection of the accident scene
   D. the victim being put into an ambulance

7. The opening paragraph of a news article is known as the 7.____
   A. topic   B. subhead   C. leader   D. lede

45

8. A copy editor assigned to work on a fiction novel is unsure if a particular phrase should be set in italics. To check if italics are appropriate, the editor should
    A. refer to the Chicago Manual of Style
    B. e-mail an excerpt to a fellow editor for guidance
    C. confer with the writer and come to an agreement on proper style
    D. refer to the Associated Press Stylebook

8.____

9. In publishing software, *bleed* is a term related to
    A. graphic images
    B. run-on sentences
    C. red editing marks
    D. page layout

9.____

10. A picture in a newspaper is accompanied by a description that reads:
    OLD MAN WINTER RETURNS
    Timmy Harris, 8, builds a snowman at Laramie Park on the first afternoon of winter.

    In newspaper parlance, the phrase "Old Man Winter Returns" is known as the
    A. headline   B. caption   C. cutline   D. subhead

10.____

Questions 11-20.

DIRECTIONS: In Questions 11 through 20, print in the space at the right the capital letter immediately preceding the word or phrase which is CLOSEST in meaning to that of the capitalized letter.

11. BIBLIOPHILE
    A. appendix
    B. library
    C. list of references
    D. lover of books

11.____

12. SACERDOTAL
    A. penitential   B. priestly   C. reminiscent   D. spiritual

12.____

13. FLAGELLATE
    A. communicate by signals
    B. pillage
    C. play the flute
    D. scourge

13.____

14. SAGA
    A. epoch   B. hero   C. inscription   D. legend

14.____

15. APOCRYPHAL
    A. annotated   B. orthodox   C. unauthentic   D. visionary

15.____

16. CAVIL
    A. make captious objection
    B. punish severely
    C. render just praise
    D. warn emphatically

16.____

17. SUPERFLUOUS
    A. impressive
    B. formidable
    C. unnecessary
    D. increasing

17.____

18. ACCORD
    A. deceit   B. agreement   C. tension   D. comfort

19. RUE
    A. abandon   B. despair   C. repent   D. stain

20. CAPRICIOUS
    A. impulsive
    B. intimidating
    C. captivating
    D. unwholesome

21. Of the following, the grammatically CORRECT sentence is:
    A. Neither the mayor nor the city clerk are willing to talk.
    B. Neither the mayor nor the city clerk is willing to talk.
    C. Neither the mayor or the city clerk are willing to talk.
    D. Neither the mayor or the city clerk is willing to talk.

22. Of the following, the grammatically CORRECT sentence is:
    A. Being that he is that kind of boy, cooperation cannot be expected.
    B. He interviewed people who he thought had something to say.
    C. Stop whomever enters the building regardless of rank or office held.
    D. Passing through the countryside, the scenery pleased us.

23. Of the following, the grammatically CORRECT sentence is:
    A. The childrens' shoes were in their closet.
    B. The children's shoes were in their closet.
    C. The childs' shoes were in their closest.
    D. The childs' shoes were in his closet.

24. Of the following, the grammatically INCORRECT sentence is:
    A. Dissatisfaction with the theoretical bases and practical workings of the general property tax has given rise to two movements of tax reform.
    B. Let the book lie on the table.
    C. Since the department is reducing its number of employees is not proof that they are not needed.
    D. Who do you think will be selected for the position?

25. Of the following, the grammatically INCORRECT sentence is:
    A. Application of the principles discovered during those experiments have been of great value to mankind.
    B. Every one of the editorial assistants proved his worth without exception.
    C. State regulation of morals aids in the protection of the family.
    D. Working when one is tired does not yield the best results.

KEY (CORRECT ANSWERS)

1.	A	11.	D
2.	A	12.	B
3.	B	13.	D
4.	C	14.	D
5.	C	15.	C
6.	C	16.	A
7.	D	17.	C
8.	A	18.	B
9.	D	19.	C
10.	B	20.	A

21. B
22. B
23. B
24. C
25. A

EXAMINATION SECTION
TEST 1

DIRECTIONS: Each question or incomplete statement is followed by several suggested answers or completions. Select the one that BEST answers the question or completes the statement. *PRINT THE LETTER OF THE CORRECT ANSWER IN THE SPACE AT THE RIGHT.*

1. Of the following, the order in which a piece of local copy is MOST likely to flow is
   A. city editor, copy reader, compositor
   B. compositor, city editor, copy reader
   C. compositor, copy reader, city editor
   D. copy reader, compositor, city editor

   1.____

2. The one who edits copy and writes headlines at a newspaper copy desk is USUALLY called a
   A. copy cutter   B. copy holder   C. copy editor   D. layout tech

   2.____

3. An editorial assistant is asked to contact a representative of a cosmetics company for general information about a product that will be featured in an upcoming lifestyle feature. The assistant arranges a video call with an influencer who has promoted the product on Instagram. This is _____ because _____.
   A. *appropriate*; the influencer needs to know the product in depth in order to heavily promote it
   B. *appropriate*; influencers are typically employed by the businesses they promote and are representatives of the company
   C. *inappropriate*; influencers as a whole cannot be trusted
   D. *inappropriate*; influencers are typically not affiliated with the businesses they promote and are not representatives of the company

   3.____

4. As a defense against libel, one could claim that a statement was quoted from the CONGRESSIONAL RECORD and, therefore, was a(n)
   A. indirect quotation   B. personal comment
   C. privileged statement   D. reporter's prerogative

   4.____

5. In order to have an illustration continue off the edge of a page, you would instruct the printer to
   A. bleed   B. cutoff   C. justify   D. mortise

   5.____

6. The description that accompanies a photograph or diagram is called a(n)
   A. cutline   B. flag   C. overhead   D. underhead

   6.____

7. A headline stretching across all columns of a page is called a
   A. bank   B. banner   C. cross line   D. drop line

   7.____

8. You would expect a headline that is flush right and left to
   A. comprise two or more decks
   B. fill the entire line
   C. have black em borders at both ends
   D. have two ems of white space on both left and right hand sides

   8.____

9. A headline that carries a story continued from another page is known as a
   A. break   B. filler   C. jump   D. read-in

   9.____

10. The secondary part of a headline is a
    A. byline   B. deck   C. slug   D. subhead

    10.____

11. A single piece of type that includes two or more letters is called
    A. dingbat   B. linotype   C. logotype   D. nonpareil

    11.____

12. The one of the following terms that refers to the stylized name of a newspaper or magazine on the publication's first page is
    A. block   B. mast   C. title   D. flag

    12.____

13. Type left over and unused after a magazine has been sent to press is called
    A. folo copy   B. make-ready   C. overset   D. quoin

    13.____

14. An upper and lower case crossline reads as follows: Dr. Doe Appointed.
    The unit count of this crossline is
    A. 14½   B. 16   C. 18   D. 19

    14.____

15. An editor reads the following sentence: "Dr. Perry's wife Margie said the longtime pediatrician was proud to be apart of the West Lake community."
    The editor should revise this sentence because
    A. family members should not be quoted unless absolutely necessary
    B. the sentence should be in the present tense
    C. using "Dr. Perry" and "pediatrician" is redundant
    D. there is a misspelling

    15.____

16. When copy for a standard-size newspaper is returned with instructions to *cut to 1 col.*, the number of words should be reduced to APPROXIMATELY
    A. 500   B. 1000   C. 1500   D. 2000

    16.____

17. A proofreader writes and circles the abbreviation *sc* in the margin, meaning that the text should be
    A. bold   B. resized   C. stricken   D. set in small caps

    17.____

18. When a story is continued on a second page, the copyreader marks the bottom of the first page with
    A. ##   B. -30-   C. insuff.   D. more

    18.____

19. The copyreader's symbol which is used to indicate that a subhead should be centered is
    A. ⌊   B. ⌋   C. ⌞⌟   D. ⌐⌐

    19.____

50

3 (#1)

20. The copyreader's symbol which is used to indicate the start of a paragraph is   20._____

A. ⌊   B. #   C. ○   D. ∼

Questions 21-25.

DIRECTIONS: Questions 21 through 25 consist of four pairs of words each. Some of the words are spelled correctly; others are spelled incorrectly. For each question, indicate in the space at the right the letter preceding that pair of words in which BOTH words are spelled CORRECTLY.

21. A. hygienic, inviegle   B. omniscience, pittance   21._____
    C. plagarize, nullify   D. seargent, perilous

22. A. auxilary, existence   B. pronounciation, baccalaureate 22._____
    C. ignominy, indegence   D. suable, baccalaureate

23. A. discreet, inaudible   B. hypocricy, onerous   23._____
    C. liquidate, maintainance   D. transparancy, onerous

24. A. facility, stimulent   B. frugel, sanitary   24._____
    C. monetary, prefatory   D. punctileous, credentials

25. A. bankruptsy, perceptible   B. disuade, resilient   25._____
    C. exhilerate, expectancy   D. panegyric, disparate

KEY (CORRECT ANSWERS)

1.	A		11.	C
2.	C		12.	D
3.	D		13.	C
4.	C		14.	B
5.	A		15.	D
6.	A		16.	B
7.	B		17.	D
8.	B		18.	D
9.	C		19.	C
10.	B		20.	A

21. B
22. D
23. A
24. C
25. D

TEST 2

DIRECTIONS: Each question or incomplete statement is followed by several suggested answers or completions. Select the one that BEST answers the question or completes the statement. *PRINT THE LETTER OF THE CORRECT ANSWER IN THE SPACE AT THE RIGHT.*

1. Spot news stories are USUALLY written 1.____
   A. as feature articles
   B. in inverted pyramid style
   C. to fill inside pages
   D. with chronological organization

2. Which of the following contains no punctuation or grammar error?
   A. Adams the second American president, hailed from Massachusetts.
   B. Grant's-Tomb can be found in Manhattan near the Hudson River.
   C. Washington's Mount Vernon, is set on a hill near the Potomac.
   D. Jefferson's estate, Monticello, is located in Virginia.

3. A good reporter avoids taking extensive notes during an interview because 3.____
   A. accuracy is of secondary importance in reporting an interview
   B. a rewrite editor may actually write the story
   C. this may mark the reporter as an amateur
   D. this may distract the person being interviewed

4. A reporter is present at a function where a distinguished person is scheduled 4.____
   to speak. He has a complete advance copy of the text.
   During the speech, the reporter could BEST use his time to
   A. follow the text to see if the speaker deviates from it
   B. organize the material of the text for later writing
   C. take direct quotations from the text
   D. write headlines for the story

5. A news story written in an inverted pyramid form is one in which the 5.____
   A. climax is reached at the end of the story
   B. climax is reached near the middle of the story
   C. facts are arranged in chronological order of occurrence
   D. facts are arranged in descending order of reader interest

6. According to the AP Stylebook, in a news story, the first mention of the 6.____
   former Catholic Cardinal of New York should be written as
   A. Cardinal Terence Cook
   B. Terence Cardinal Cook
   C. The Rt. Rev. Terence Cook
   D. The Very Rev. Terence Cook

7. Of the following pairs, the one that is an example of a homophone is 7.____
   A. sing; sang
   B. ring (verb); ring (noun)
   C. inside; outside
   D. baring; bearing

8. The MOST common type of lede on newspaper stories is the _____ lede.
   A. astonisher
   B. quotation
   C. summary
   D. suspended-interest

9. The one of the following terms which does NOT designate a story accompanying a report of a major news event is
   A. precede
   B. shirt tail
   C. sidebar
   D. subhead

10. A second-day story is also known as a
    A. filler
    B. flimsy
    C. follow copy
    D. follow story

11. A phrase or word used on copy to identify additional pages of a news story is called a
    A. headline
    B. slot
    C. slug
    D. stamp

12. A *tear sheet* is a
    A. carbon copy of a story
    B. galley proof of a story
    C. page proof of a publication
    D. printed page from a publication

13. If you were told to *boil* a story, you would
    A. expand with editorial comment
    B. present only essential facts
    C. try to keep it a *scoop*
    D. write a large headline spread

14. If a reporter went to the *morgue*, he would be seeing
    A. carbon copies of an article he had just written
    B. clippings on the subject he was writing about
    C. galley proofs of a recently completed article
    D. incoming press association teletype copy

15. A beat reporter's *future book* is a
    A. chronological listing on expected events on his beat
    B. list of news sources on his beat
    C. novel he eventually hopes to write
    D. schedule of assignments kept for editor of editorial page

16. To a magazine editor, the term *query* means a
    A. letter outlining an article idea
    B. personal request for conference with the editor
    C. request for an advance
    D. rough draft of an article

17. The one of the following that is NOT on the editorial staff of a large metropolitan newspaper is the
    A. copyreader
    B. photographer
    C. proofreader
    D. rewrite man

18. The name given to a newspaper contributor who writes, edits or provides photography on a freelance basis is
    A. bulldog   B. beat   C. stringer   D. pooler

    18.____

19. A writer is assigned to cover the local school district. In this case, the school district is known as the writer's
    A. territory   B. beat   C. press pool   D. lead

    19.____

20. Information that is no longer under copyright protection is considered part of the
    A. free press
    B. free speech entitlement
    C. public record
    D. public domain

    20.____

KEY (CORRECT ANSWERS)

1.	B		11.	C
2.	D		12.	D
3.	D		13.	B
4.	A		14.	B
5.	D		15.	A
6.	A		16.	A
7.	D		17.	C
8.	C		18.	C
9.	D		19.	B
10.	D		20.	D

EXAMINATION SECTION
TEST 1

DIRECTIONS: Each question or incomplete statement is followed by several suggested answers or completions. Select the one that BEST answers the question or completes the statement. *PRINT THE LETTER OF THE CORRECT ANSWER IN THE SPACE AT THE RIGHT.*

1. The basic data-entry units that make up a spreadsheet are called
   A. boxes   B. cells   C. sheets   D. tabs

2. You are assigned the task of creating a brochure that includes descriptions and images of the seasonal amenities available to town residents. The best software to use to create this brochure is
   A. Microsoft PowerPoint
   B. Adobe InDesign
   C. Google Drive
   D. Adobe Acrobat

3. The term *duplex* refers to
   A. prints with more than two colors
   B. tabloid-style newspapers
   C. double-spaced printing
   D. two-sided printing

4. Copyright law should be considered when an editor is
   A. thinking of synonyms that would enhance a magazine piece
   B. searching for images to run in a blog post
   C. deciding whether or not to use an anonymous source
   D. all of the above

5. Libel and slander both relate to the spread of false information, but differ in that libelous statements are _____ and slanderous statements are _____.
   A. violent; threatening
   B. in newspapers; on the internet
   C. written; spoken
   D. spoken; written

6. The proofreading mark used to indicate that text or punctuation should be inserted in a particular place is called a(n)
   A. asterisk   B. pound sign   C. caret   D. slash

7. A social media assistant is told to put up a Facebook post the day before a youth video-game tournament at the local library. To best promote the tournament and generate excitement, the body of the post should read
   A. "It's Gamer Day Eve! Come on down tomorrow for a fun-filled day playing your favorite games!"
   B. "VIDEO GAMES TOMORROW! SEE YOU THERE!!!"
   C. "GAME...ON!!! First annual City Library Gamer Day Tourney begins in T-minus 24 hours! See you at 10 a.m.!"
   D. "Mayor Johnson wishes all participants in tomorrow's Gamer Day Tourney at City Library the best of luck, and new high scores for all!"

55

8. It is your job to post videos on Instagram of the day's leading news stories. Each post must include an excerpt from the news article, and a short headline should appear as a banner over the footage.
Which of the following headlines is correct in both style and grammar?
   A. TOWN COUNSEL APPROVES PERMIT FOR NEW DISTILLERY
   B. TOWN COUNSEL ISSUES PERMIT FOR LOCAL BREWERY
   C. TOWN COUNCIL APPROVED PERMIT FOR NEW DISTILLERY
   D. TOWN COUNCIL ISSUES PERMIT FOR NEW DISTILLERY

9. To assure credibility and avoid hostility, a public relations specialist MUST
   A. make certain the message is truthful, not evasive or exaggerated
   B. make sure the message contains some dire consequences, if ignored
   C. repeat the message often enough to that it cannot be ignored
   D. try to reach as many people and groups as possible

10. The public relations specialist MUST be prepared to assume that members of an audience
    A. may have developed attitudes toward proposals, whether favorable, neutral or unfavorable
    B. will be immediately hostile
    C. will consider any proposals with an open mind
    D. will invariably need an introduction to the subject

11. To a copy editor, *slug* means
    A. first sentence of a story
    B. identification of a story
    C. size of type in which a story is to be set
    D. the story needs punch or drive

12. You are assigned to write the photo cutline for a cover story about new local shops in the Sunday Business section. The photo shows the owner of a new coffeehouse brewing espresso as a customer waits at the register.
The cutline should include all of the following information EXCEPT the
    A. name of the owner   B. location of the coffeehouse
    C. name of the coffeehouse   D. name of the customer

13. When covering political events, a group of reporters might distribute quotes and relevant information to a larger contingent of journalists. These reporters are called
    A. political correspondents   B. news desk reporters
    C. distributing journalists   D. pool reporters

14. The lede is the MOST important part of a news story.
It should
    A. attract the reader
    B. give all the facts immediately
    C. start with the source of the story
    D. start with the time of the story

15. There are several acceptable ways of writing a news story. 15.____
It should USUALLY be written
    A. as facts become known, regardless of chronology
    B. chronologically
    C. in order of decreasing importance or interest
    D. so that details come at the end

16. A reporter assigned to cover a scheduled broadcast speech GENERALLY 16.____
    A. gets shorthand notes afterwards
    B. takes shorthand notes himself
    C. receives an advance copy
    D. writes his story from the radio or television broadcast

17. A reporter is told that an interview has been set up for him for the next day with 17.____
an authority on earthquakes. He is given the name and affiliation of the
authority and the location and time of the interview.
His NEXT step is to
    A. bring along a seismology expert to the interview
    B. do research on seismology and get biographical data on the interviewee
    C. try to arrange a luncheon date with the interviewee
    D. verify time and place of interview

18. When a story is worth handling on a continuing basis, even if no added news is 18.____
available, a writer will be asked to
    A. call the sources on deadline and make sure no facts are changed
    B. rearrange the story, putting other details in the lead
    C. shorten the story
    D. write a *second day* lead

19. There are almost as many techniques of interviewing as there are interviewers. 19.____
Of the following, the LEAST objectionable method is to
    A. ask if interviewee minds being quoted
    B. make occasional notes as important topics come up
    C. take notes unobtrusively
    D. take shorthand notes of every word

20. There are many differences between feature and news stories. 20.____
The single MOST important difference is that
    A. features are longer than news stories
    B. features emphasize the unusual; news stories the significant
    C. features ignore facts that news stories cannot
    D. news stories are more timely than features

Questions 21-25.

DIRECTIONS: In each of Questions 21 through 25, only one of the four sentences conforms to standards of correct usage. The other three contain errors in grammar, diction or punctuation. Select the option in each question which conforms to standards of correct usage. Consider an option correct if it contains none of the errors mentioned above, even though there may be other correct ways of expressing the same thought.

21. A. Because he was ill was no excuse for his behavior. 21.____
    B. I insist that he see a lawyer before he goes to trial.
    C. He said "that he had not intended to go."
    D. He wasn't out of the office only three days.

22. A. He came to the station and pays a porter to carry his bags into the train. 22.____
    B. I should have liked to live in medieval times.
    C. My father was born in Linville. A little country town where everyone knows everyone else.
    D. The car, which is parked across the street, is disabled.

23. A. He asked the desk clerk for a clean, quiet, room. 23.____
    B. I expected James to be lonesome and that he would want to go home.
    C. I have stopped worrying because I have heard nothing further on the subject.
    D. If the board of directors controls the company, they may take actions which are disapproved by the stockholders.

24. A. Each of the players knew their place. 24.____
    B. He whom you saw on the stage is the son of an actor.
    C. Susan is the smartest of the twin sisters.
    D. Who ever thought of him winning both prizes?

25. A. An outstanding trait of early man was their reliance on omens. 25.____
    B. Because I had never been there before.
    C. Neither Mr. Jones nor Mr. Smith has completed his work.
    D. While eating my dinner, a dog came to the window.

KEY (CORRECT ANSWERS)

1.	B	11.	B
2.	B	12.	D
3.	D	13.	D
4.	B	14.	A
5.	C	15.	C
6.	C	16.	C
7.	C	17.	B
8.	D	18.	D
9.	A	19.	C
10.	A	20.	B

21. B
22. B
23. C
24. B
25. C

TEST 2

DIRECTIONS: Each question or incomplete statement is followed by several suggested answers or completions. Select the one that BEST answers the question or completes the statement. *PRINT THE LETTER OF THE CORRECT ANSWER IN THE SPACE AT THE RIGHT.*

1. In a pre-edited news article or press release, ____ indicates the end of text. 1.____
   A. -30- B. -end- C. stet D. -XX-

2. The term *double truck* is used to describe 2.____
   A. a two-column headline
   B. the first page of the second section
   C. two adjacent pages made up as one
   D. two pictures combined into a single picture

3. To indicate that a correction should be ignored and text left as is, an editor should use the notation 3.____
   A. stet B. as/is C. -#- D. check

4. As a copy editor, you are assigned to edit an article about the local high school football team's summer training camp. The lede of the article reads: 4.____
   "Practice makes perfect, and based on early showing at camp, Marlboro might be in line for its finest season in a decade."
   This article should be sent back to the writer for revisions because
   A. clichés should be avoided in news articles, especially in the lede
   B. technically it's not accurate that practice makes perfect
   C. few readers are familiar with the history of the team
   D. the opinion of the writer is not relevant in a news article

5. The terms *vector* and *PNG* refer to 5.____
   A. peripheral devices
   B. the first word processors
   C. font packages
   D. computer graphics

6. The technique of trimming a photo to be used in a news story is known as 6.____
   A. casting off B. cropping C. routing D. scaling down

7. Which of the following fonts would be most suitable for use in the website version of a news article? 7.____
   A. Helvetica B. Baskerville C. Garamond D. Comic Sans

8. If the same article from question #7 is to be read in the print edition of the newspaper, the most suitable serif font would be 8.____
   A. Arial B. Times C. Verdana D. Copperplate

9. In typography, the number of points to an inch is APPROXIMATELY 9.____
   A. 12 B. 48 C. 72 D. 96

10. All variants of a particular type design are said to belong to the same 10.____
    A. family B. font C. quad D. run

11. Old English is in a class of type known as
    A. black letter   B. italic   C. roman   D. script

12. Which of the following is a sans serif font?
    A. Baskerville   B. Bodoni   C. Verdana   D. Garamond

13. The one of the following that is NOT associated with typography is
    A. kerning   B. cropping   C. leading   D. tracking

14. Of the following, the term that is NOT associated with the printing process is
    A. collate   B. duplex   C. export   D. offset

15. A large capital letter used as block text at the start of a paragraph is called a
    A. letter block   B. drop cap   C. drophead   D. subhead

16. A method of printing in which a relief process is used is
    A. intaglio   B. letter press   C. lithography   D. offset

17. A screened engraving of a photograph is known as
    A. intaglio   B. letter press   C. lithography   D. offset

18. In typography, the term used for arranging type in lines so that all the lines in a column are even is
    A. conversion   B. furnishing   C. justifying   D. leading

19. The front page of THE NEW YORK TIMES most frequently exemplifies the make-up known as
    A. balanced
    B. circus
    C. focus
    D. hanging indentation

20. Information about a newspaper's publisher, offices and subscription rates are typically found
    A. on the editorial page
    B. in the masthead
    C. beneath the lead story
    D. in the classified section

21. The word *stet* tells the printer to
    A. capitalize all letters in the phrase
    B. omit the phrase
    C. reinstate the phrase marked out
    D. set the marked phrase in italics

22. In proofreading, the symbol ✓✓✓ indicates that the printer should
    A. check with original manuscript
    B. correct faulty spacing
    C. insert quotation marks
    D. straighten lines

23. A proofreader indicates a *bad* or *defective letter* by the symbol   23.____
    A. ✗   B. ▢   C. ↶   D. ♯

24. The proofreading symbol meaning *close up partly but leave some space* is   24.____
    A. (/)   B. ⊙   C. ♯̂   D. ▢

25. A proof containing the misspelling *Beleive* should be marked   25.____
    A. tr   B. wf   C. ⊙   D. ⌐

KEY (CORRECT ANSWERS)

1.	A		11.	A
2.	C		12.	C
3.	A		13.	B
4.	A		14.	C
5.	D		15.	B
6.	B		16.	B
7.	A		17.	A
8.	B		18.	C
9.	C		19.	A
10.	A		20.	B

21. C
22. B
23. A
24. C
25. A

EXAMINATION SECTION
TEST 1

DIRECTIONS: Each question or incomplete statement is followed by several suggested answers or completions. Select the one that BEST answers the question or completes the statement. *PRINT THE LETTER OF THE CORRECT ANSWER IN THE SPACE AT THE RIGHT.*

1. In public agencies, communications should be based PRIMARILY on a
    A. two-way flow from the top down and from the bottom up, most of which should be given in writing to avoid ambiguity
    B. multi-direction flow among all levels and with outside persons
    C. rapid, internal one-way flow from the top down
    D. two-way flow of information, most of which should be given orally for purposes of clarity

2. In some organizations, changes in policy or procedures are often communicated by word of mouth from supervisors to employees with no prior discussion or exchange of viewpoints with employees.
   This procedure often produces employee dissatisfaction CHIEFLY because
    A. information is mostly unusable since a considerable amount of time is required to transmit information
    B. lower-level supervisors tend to be excessively concerned with minor details
    C. management has failed to seek employees' advice before making changes
    D. valuable staff time is lost between decision-making and the implementation of decisions

3. For good letter writing, you should try to visualize the person to whom you are writing, especially if you know him.
   Of the following rules, it is LEAST helpful in such visualization to think of
    A. the person's likes and dislikes, his concerns, and his needs
    B. what you would be likely to say if speaking in person
    C. what you would expect to be asked if speaking in person
    D. your official position in order to be certain that your words are proper

4. One approach to good informal letter writing is to make letters and conversational.
   All of the following practices will usually help to do this EXCEPT:
    A. If possible, use a style which is similar to the style used when speaking
    B. Substitute phrases for single words (e.g., *at the present time* for *now*)
    C. Use contractions of words (e.g., *you're* for *you are*)
    D. Use ordinary vocabulary when possible

5. All of the following rules will aid in producing clarity in report-writing EXCEPT:
   A. Give specific details or examples, if possible
   B. Keep related words close together in each sentence
   C. Present information in sequential order
   D. Put several thoughts or ideas in each paragraph

6. The one of the following statements about public relations which is MOST accurate is that
   A. in the long run, appearance gains better results than performance
   B. objectivity is decreased if outside public relations consultants are employed
   C. public relations is the responsibility of every employee
   D. public relations should be based on a formal publicity program

7. The form of communication which is usually considered to be MOST personally directed to the intended recipient is the
   A. brochure   B. film   C. letter   D. radio

8. In general, a document that presents an organization's views or opinions on a particular topic is MOST accurately known as a
   A. tear sheet   B. position paper
   C. flyer   D. journal

9. Assume that you have been asked to speak before an organization of persons who oppose a newly announced program in which you are involved. You feel tense about talking to this group.
   Which of the following rules generally would be MOST useful in gaining rapport when speaking before the audience?
   A. Impress them with your experience
   B. Stress all areas of disagreement
   C. Talk to the group as to one person
   D. Use formal grammar and language

10. An organization must have an effective public relations program since, at its best, public relations is a bridge to change.
    All of the following statements about communication and human behavior have validity EXCEPT:
    A. People are more likely to talk about controversial matters with like-minded people than with those holding other views
    B. The earlier an experience, the more powerful its effect since it influences how later experiences will be interpreted
    C. In periods of social tension, official sources gain increased believability
    D. Those who are already interested in a topic are the ones who are most open to receive new communications about it

11. An employee should be encouraged to talk easily and frankly when he is dealing with his supervisor.
    In order to encourage such free communication, it would be MOST appropriate for a supervisor to behave in a(n)
    A. sincere manner; assure the employee that you will deal with him honestly and openly
    B. official manner; you are a supervisor and must always act formally with subordinates
    C. investigative manner; you must probe and question to get to a basis of trust
    D. unemotional manner; the employee's emotions and background should play no part in your dealings with him

11.____

12. Research findings show that an increase in free communication within an agency GENERALLY results in which one of the following?
    A. Improved morale and productivity
    B. Increased promotional opportunities
    C. An increase in authority
    D. A spirit of honesty

12.____

13. Assume that you are a supervisor and your superiors have given you a new-type procedure to be followed.
    Before passing this information on to your subordinates, the one of the following actions that you should take FIRST is to
    A. ask your superiors to send out a memorandum to the entire staff
    B. clarify the procedure in your own mind
    C. set up a training course to provide instruction on the new procedure
    D. write a memorandum to your subordinates

13.____

14. Communication is necessary for an organization to be effective.
    The one of the following which is LEAST important for most communication systems is that
    A. messages are sent quickly and directly to the person who needs them to operate
    B. information should be conveyed understandably and accurately
    C. the method used to transmit information should be kept secret so that security can be maintained
    D. senders of messages must know how their messages are received and acted upon

14.____

15. Which one of the following is the CHIEF advantage of listening willingly to subordinates and encouraging them to talk freely and honestly?
    It
    A. reveals to supervisors the degree to which ideas that are passed down are accepted by subordinates
    B. reduces the participation of subordinates in the operation of the department
    C. encourages subordinates to try for promotion
    D. enables supervisors to learn more readily what the *grapevine* is saying

15.____

16. A supervisor may be informed through either oral or written reports. 16.____
Which one of the following is an ADVANTAGE of using oral reports?
    A. There is no need for a formal record of the report.
    B. An exact duplicate of the report is not easily transmitted to others.
    C. A good oral report requires little time for preparation.
    D. An oral report involves two-way communication between a subordinate and his supervisor.

17. Of the following, the MOST important reason why supervisors should communicate effectively with the public is to 17.____
    A. improve the public's understanding of information that is important for them to know
    B. establish a friendly relationship
    C. obtain information about the kinds of people who come to the agency
    D. convince the public that services are adequate

18. Supervisors should generally NOT use phrases like *too hard*, *too easy*, and *a lot* PRINCIPALLY because such phrases 18.____
    A. may be offensive to some minority groups
    B. are too informal
    C. mean different things to different people
    D. are difficult to remember

19. The ability to communicate clearly and concisely is an important element in effective leadership. 19.____
Which of the following statements about oral and written communication is GENERALLY true?
    A. Oral communication is more time-consuming.
    B. Written communication is more likely to be misinterpreted.
    C. Oral communication is useful only in emergencies.
    D. Written communication is useful mainly when giving information to fewer than twenty people.

20. Rumors can often have harmful and disruptive effects on an organization. 20.____
Which one of the following is the BEST way to prevent rumors from becoming a problem?
    A. Refuse to act on rumors, thereby making them less believable.
    B. Increase the amount of information passed along by the *grapevine*.
    C. Distribute as much factual information as possible.
    D. Provide training in report writing.

21. Suppose that a subordinate asks you about a rumor he has heard. The rumor deals with a subject which your superiors consider *confidential*. 21.____
Which of the following BEST describes how you should answer the subordinate? Tell

A. the subordinate that you don't make the rules and that he should speak to higher ranking officials
B. the subordinate that you will ask your superior for information
C. him only that you cannot comment on the matter
D. him the rumor is not true

22. Supervisors often find it difficult to *get their message across* when instructing newly appointed employees in their various duties.
The MAIN reason for this is generally that the
    A. duties of the employees have increased
    B. supervisor is often so expert in his area that he fails to see it from the learner's point of view
    C. supervisor adapts his instruction to the slowest learner in the group
    D. new employees are younger, less concerned with job security and more interested in fringe benefits

23. Assume that you are discussing a job problem with an employee under your supervision. During the discussion, you see that the man's eyes are turning away from you and that he is not paying attention.
In order to get the man's attention, you should FIRST
    A. ask him to look you in the eye
    B. talk to him about sports
    C. tell him he is being very rude
    D. change your tone of voice

24. As a supervisor, you may find it necessary to conduct meetings with your subordinates.
Of the following, which would be MOST helpful in assuring that a meeting accomplishes the purpose for which it was called?
    A. Give notice of the conclusions you would like to reach at the start of the meeting.
    B. Delay the start of the meeting until everyone is present.
    C. Write down points to be discussed in proper sequence.
    D. Make sure everyone is clear on whatever conclusions have been reached and on what must be done after the meeting.

25. Every supervisor will occasionally be called upon to deliver a reprimand to a subordinate. If done properly, this can greatly help an employee improve his performance.
Which one of the following is NOT a good practice to follow when giving a reprimand?
    A. Maintain your composure and temper
    B. Reprimand a subordinate in the presence of other employees so they can learn the same lesson
    C. Try to understand why the employee was not able to perform satisfactorily
    D. Let your knowledge of the man involved determine the exact nature of the reprimand

KEY (CORRECT ANSWERS)

1.	C	11.	A
2.	B	12.	A
3.	D	13.	B
4.	B	14.	C
5.	D	15.	A
6.	C	16.	D
7.	C	17.	A
8.	B	18.	C
9.	C	19.	B
10.	C	20.	C

21.	B
22.	B
23.	D
24.	D
25.	B

TEST 2

DIRECTIONS: Each question or incomplete statement is followed by several suggested answers or completions. Select the one that BEST answers the question or completes the statement. *PRINT THE LETTER OF THE CORRECT ANSWER IN THE SPACE AT THE RIGHT.*

1. Usually one thinks of communication as a single step, essentially that of transmitting an idea.
   Actually, however, this is only part of a total process, the FIRST step of which should be
   A. the prompt dissemination of the idea to those who may be affected by it
   B. motivating those affected to take the required action
   C. clarifying the idea in one's own mind
   D. deciding to whom the idea is to be communicated

   1.____

2. Research studies on patterns of informal communication have concluded that most individuals in a group tend to be passive recipients of news, while a few make it their business to spread it around in an organization.
   With this conclusion in mind, it would be MOST correct for the supervisor to attempt to identify these few individuals and
   A. give them the complete facts on important matters in advance of others
   B. inform the other subordinates of the identity of these few individuals so that their influence may be minimized
   C. keep them straight on the facts on important matters
   D. warn them to cease passing along any information to others

   2.____

3. The one of the following which is the PRINCIPAL advantage of making an oral report is that it
   A. affords an immediate opportunity for two-way communication between the subordinate and superior
   B. is an easy method for the superior to use in transmitting information to others of equal rank
   C. saves the time of all concerned
   D. permits more precise pinpointing of praise or blame by means of follow-up questions by the superior

   3.____

4. An agency may sometimes undertake a public relations program of a defensive nature.
   With reference to the use of defensive public relations, it would be MOST correct to state that it
   A. is bound to be ineffective since defensive statements, even though supported by factual data, can never hope to even partly overcome the effects of prior unfavorable attacks
   B. proves that the agency has failed to establish good relationships with newspapers, radio stations, or other means of publicity

   4.____

C. shows that the upper echelons of the agency have failed to develop sound public relations procedures and techniques
D. is sometimes required to aid morale by protecting the agency from unjustified criticism and misunderstanding of policies or procedures

5. Of the following factors which contribute to possible undesirable public attitudes towards an agency, the one which is MOST susceptible to being changed by the efforts of the individual employee in an organization is that
    A. enforcement of unpopular regulations as offended many individuals
    B. the organization itself has an unsatisfactory reputation
    C. the public is not interested in agency matters
    D. there are many errors in judgment committed by individual subordinates

5.____

6. It is not enough for an agency's services to be of a high quality; attention must also be given to the acceptability of these services to the general public.
This statement is GENERALLY
    A. *false*; a superior quality of service automatically wins public support
    B. *true*; the agency cannot generally progress beyond the understanding and support of the public
    C. *false*; the acceptance by the public of agency services determines their quality
    D. *true*; the agency is generally unable to engage in any effective enforcement activity without public support

6.____

7. Sustained agency participation in a program sponsored by a community organization is MOST justified when
    A. the achievement of agency objectives in some area depends partly on the activity of this organization
    B. the community organization is attempting to widen the base of participation in all community affairs
    C. the agency is uncertain as to what the community wants
    D. the agency is uncertain as to what the community wants

7.____

8. Of the following, the LEAST likely way in which a records system may serve a supervisor is in
    A. developing a sympathetic and cooperative public attitude toward the agency
    B. improving the quality of supervision by permitting a check on the accomplishment of subordinates
    C. permit a precise prediction of the exact incidences in specific categories for the following year
    D. helping to take the guesswork out of the distribution of the agency

8.____

9. Assuming that the *grapevine* in any organization is virtually indestructible, the one of the following which it is MOST important for management to understand is:
    A. What is being spread by means of the *grapevine* and the reason for spreading it
    B. What is being spread by means of the *grapevine* and how it is being spread
    C. Who is involved in spreading the information that is on the *grapevine*
    D. Why those who are involved in spreading the information are doing so

9._____

10. When the supervisor writes a report concerning an investigation to which he has been assigned, it should be LEAST intended to provide
    A. a permanent official record of relevant information gathered
    B. a summary of case findings limited to facts which tend to indicate the guilt of a suspect
    C. a statement of the facts on which higher authorities may base a corrective or disciplinary action
    D. other investigators with information so that they may continue with other phases of the investigation

10._____

11. In survey work, questionnaires rather than interviews are sometimes used. The one of the following which is a DISADVANTAGE of the questionnaire method as compared with the interview is the
    A. difficulty of accurately interpreting the results
    B. problem of maintaining anonymity of the participant
    C. fact that it is relatively uneconomical
    D. requirement of special training for the distribution of questionnaires

11._____

12. in his contacts with the public, an employee should attempt to create a good climate of support for his agency.
    This statement is GENERALLY
    A. *false*; such attempts are clearly beyond the scope of his responsibility
    B. *true*; employees of an agency who come in contact with the public have the opportunity to affect public relations
    C. *false*; such activity should be restricted to supervisors trained in public relations techniques
    D. *true*; the future expansion of the agency depends to a great extent on continued public support of the agency

12._____

13. The repeated use by a supervisor of a call for volunteers to get a job done is objectionable MAINLY because it
    A. may create a feeling of animosity between the volunteers and the non-volunteers
    B. may indicate that the supervisor is avoiding responsibility for making assignments which will be most productive
    C. is an indication that the supervisor is not familiar with the individual capabilities of his men
    D. is unfair to men who, for valid reasons, do not, or cannot volunteer

13._____

14. Of the following statements concerning subordinates' expressions to a supervisor of their opinions and feelings concerning work situations, the one which is MOST correct is that
    A. by listening and responding to such expressions the supervisor encourages the development of complaints
    B. the lack of such expressions should indicate to the supervisor that there is a high level of job satisfaction
    C. the more the supervisor listens to and responds to such expressions, the more he demonstrates lack of supervisory ability
    D. by listening and responding to such expressions, the supervisor will enable many subordinates to understand and solve their own problems on the job

14.____

15. In attempting to motivate employees, rewards are considered preferable to punishment PRIMARILY because
    A. punishment seldom has any effect on human behavior
    B. punishment usually results in decreased production
    C. supervisors find it difficult to punish
    D. rewards are more likely to result in willing cooperation

15.____

16. In an attempt to combat the low morale in his organization, a high level supervisor publicized an *open-door policy* to allow employees who wished to do so to come to him with their complaints.
    Which of the following is LEAST likely to account for the fact that no employee came in with a complaint?
    A. Employees are generally reluctant to go over the heads of their immediate supervisor.
    B. The employees did not feel that management would help them.
    C. The low morale was not due to complaints associated with the job.
    D. The employees felt that they had more to lose than to gain.

16.____

17. It is MOST desirable to use written instructions rather than oral instructions for a particular job when
    A. a mistake on the job will not be serious
    B. the job can be completed in a short time
    C. there is no need to explain the job minutely
    D. the job involves many details

17.____

18. If you receive a telephone call regarding a matter which your office does not handle, you should FIRST
    A. give the caller the telephone number of the proper office so that he can dial again
    B. offer to transfer the caller to the proper office
    C. suggest that the caller re-dial since he probably dialed incorrectly
    D. tell the caller he has reached the wrong office and then hang up

18.____

19. When you answer the telephone, the MOST important reason for identifying yourself and your organization is to
    A. give the caller time to collect his or her thoughts
    B. impress the caller with your courtesy
    C. inform the caller that he or she has reached the right number
    D. set a business-like tone at the beginning of the conversation

    19._____

20. As soon as you pick up the phone, a very angry caller begins immediately to complain about city agencies and *red tape*. He says that he has been shifted to two or three different offices. It turs out that he is seeking information which is not immediately available to you. You believe, you know, however, where it can be found.
    Which of the following actions is the BEST one for you to take?
    A. To eliminate all confusion, suggest that the caller write the agency stating explicitly what he wants.
    B. Apologize by telling the caller how busy city agencies now are, but also tell him directly that you do not have the information he needs.
    C. Ask for the caller's telephone number and assure him you will call back after you have checked further.
    D. Give the caller the name and telephone number of the person who might be able to help, but explain that you are not positive he will get results/

    20._____

21. Which of the following approaches usually provides the BEST communication in the objectives and values of a new program which is to be introduced?
    A. A general written description of the program by the program manager for review by those who share responsibility
    B. An effective verbal presentation by the program manager to those affected
    C. Development of the plan and operational approach in carrying out the program by the program manager assisted by his key subordinates
    D. Development of the plan by the program manager's supervisor

    21._____

22. What is the BEST approach for introducing change?
    A
    A. combination of written and also verbal communication to all personnel affected by the change
    B. general bulletin to all personnel
    C. meeting pointing out all the values of the new approach
    D. written directive to key personnel

    22._____

23. Of the following, committees are BEST used for
    A. advising the head of the organization
    B. improving functional work
    C. making executive decisions
    D. making specific planning decisions

    23._____

24. An effective discussion leader is one who
    A. announces the problem and his preconceived solution at the start of the discussion
    B. guides and directs the discussion according to pre-arranged outline
    C. interrupts or corrects confused participants to save time
    D. permits anyone to say anything at any time

25. The human relations movement in management theory is basically concerned with
    A. counteracting employee unrest
    B. eliminating the *time and motion* man
    C. interrelationships among individuals in organizations
    D. the psychology of the worker

KEY (CORRECT ANSWERS)

1.	C	11.	A
2.	C	12.	B
3.	A	13.	B
4.	D	14.	D
5.	D	15.	D
6.	B	16.	C
7.	A	17.	D
8.	C	18.	B
9.	A	19.	C
10.	B	20.	C

21.	C
22.	A
23.	A
24.	B
25.	C

EXAMINATION SECTION
TEST 1

DIRECTIONS: Each question or incomplete statement is followed by several suggested answers or completions. Select the one that BEST answers the question or completes the statement. *PRINT THE LETTER OF THE CORRECT ANSWER IN THE SPACE AT THE RIGHT.*

Questions 1-22.

DIRECTIONS: Read through each group of words. Indicate in the space at the right the letter of the misspelled word.

1. A. miniature   B. recession   1.____
   C. accommodate   D. supress

2. A. mortgage   B. illogical   2.____
   C. fasinate   D. pronounce

3. A. calendar   B. heros   3.____
   C. ecstasy   D. librarian

4. A. initiative   B. extraordinary   4.____
   C. villian   D. exaggerate

5. A. absence   B. sense   5.____
   C. dosn't   D. height

6. A. curiosity   B. ninety   6.____
   C. truely   D. grammar

7. A. amateur   B. definate   7.____
   C. meant   D. changeable

8. A. excellent   B. studioes   8.____
   C. achievement   D. weird

9. A. goverment   B. description   9.____
   C. sergeant   D. desirable

10. A. proceed   B. anxious   10.____
    C. neice   D. precede

11. A. environment   B. omitted   11.____
    C. apparant   D. misconstrue

12. A. comparative   B. hindrance   12.____
    C. benefited   D. unamimous

13. A. embarrass B. recommend
    C. desciple   D. argument
    13.____

14. A. sophomore B. suprintendent
    C. concievable D. disastrous
    14.____

15. A. agressive B. questionnaire
    C. occurred   D. rhythm
    15.____

16. A. peaceable B. conscientious
    C. redicule   D. deterrent
    16.____

17. A. mischievious B. writing
    C. competition   D. athletics
    17.____

18. A. auxiliary B. synonymous
    C. maneuver   D. repitition
    18.____

19. A. existence B. optomistic
    C. acquitted D. tragedy
    19.____

20. A. hypocrisy B. parrallel
    C. exhilaration D. prevalent
    20.____

21. A. convalesence B. infallible
    C. destitute   D. grotesque
    21.____

22. A. magnanimity B. asassination
    C. incorrigible D. pestilence
    22.____

Questions 23-40.

DIRECTIONS: In Questions 23 through 40, one sentence fragment contains an error in punctuation or capitalization. Indicate the letter of the INCORRECT sentence fragment and place it in the space at the right.

23. A. Despite a year's work
    B. in a well-equipped laboratory
    C. my Uncle failed to complete his research
    D. now he will never graduate.
    23.____

24. A. Gene, if you are going to sleep
    B. all afternoon I will enter
    C. that ladies' golf tournament
    D. sponsored by the Chamber of Commerce.
    24.____

25. A. Seeing the cat slink toward the barn,
    B. the farmer's wife jumped off the
    C. ladder picked up a broom, and began
    D. shouting at the top of her voice.

    25.____

26. A. Extending over southeast Idaho and
    B. northwest Wyoming, the Tetons
    C. are noted for their height; however the
    D. highest peak is actually under 14,000 feet.

    26.____

27. A. "Sarah, can you recall the name
    B. of the English queen
    C. who supposedly said, 'We are not
    D. amused?"

    27.____

28. A. My aunt's graduation present to me
    B. cost, I imagine more than she could
    C. actually afford. It's a
    D. Swiss watch with numerous features.

    28.____

29. A. On the left are examples of buildings
    B. from the Classical Period; two temples
    C. one of which was dedicated to Zeus; the
    D. Agora, a marketplace; and a large arch.

    29.____

30. A. Tired of sonic booms, the people who
    B. live near Springfield's Municipal Airport
    C. formed an anti noise organization
    D. with the amusing name of Sound Off.

    30.____

31. A. "Joe, Mrs. Sweeney said, "your family
    B. arrives Sunday. Since you'll be in
    C. the Labor Day parade, we could ask Mr.
    D. Krohn, who has a big car, to meet them."

    31.____

32. A. The plumber emerged from the basement and
    B. said, "Mr. Cohen I found the trouble in
    C. your water heater. Could you move those
    D. Schwinn bikes out of my way?"

    32.____

33. A. The President walked slowly to the
    B. podium, bowed to Edward Everett Hale
    C. the other speaker, and began his formal address:
    D. "Fourscore and seven years ago…."

    33.____

34. A. Mr. Fontana, I hope, will arrive before
    B. the beginning of the ceremonies; however,
    C. if his plane is delayed, I have a substitute
    D. speaker who can be here at a moments' notice.

    34.____

35. A. Gladys wedding dress, a satin creation,
    B. lay crumpled on the floor; her veil,
    C. torn and streaked, lay nearby. "Jilted!"
    D. shrieked Gladys. She was clearly annoyed.

35.____

36. A. Although it is poor grammar, the word
    B. hopefully has become television's newest
    C. pet expression; I hope (to use the correct
    D. form) that it will soon pass from favor.

36.____

37. A.   Plaza Apartment Hotel
    B.   103 Tower road
    C.   Hampstead, Iowa 52025
    D.   March 13, 2021

37.____

38. A. Circulation Department
    B. British History Illustrated
    C. 3000 Walnut Street
    D. Boulder Colorado 80302

38.____

39. A. Dear Sirs:
    B. Last spring I ordered a subscription to your
    C. magazine. I had read and enjoyed the May
    D. issue containing the article titled "kings."

39.____

40. A. I have not however, received a
    B. single issue. Will you check this?
    C. Sincerely,
    D. Maria Herrera

40.____

Questions 41-70.

DIRECTIONS: Questions 41 through 70 represent common grammatical concerns: subject-verb agreement, appropriate use of pronouns, and appropriate use of verbs. Read each sentence and indicate the letter of the grammatically CORRECT answer in the space at the right.

41. THE REIVERS, one of William Faulkner's last works, _____ made into a movie starring Steve McQueen.
    A. has been   B. have been   C. are being   D. were

41.____

42. He _____ on the ground, his eyes fastened on an ant slowly pushing a morsel of food toward the ant hill.
    A. layed   B. laid   C. had laid   D. lay

42.____

43. Nobody in the tri-cities _____ to admit that a flood could be disastrous.
    A. are willing   B. have been willing
    C. is willing   D. were willing

43.____

44. "_____," the senator asked, "have you convinced to run against the incumbent?"
    A. Who   B. Whom   C. Whomever   D. Womsoever

45. Of all the psychology courses that I took, Statistics 101 _____ the most demanding.
    A. was   B. are   C. is   D. were

46. Neither the conductor nor the orchestra members _____ the music to be applauded so enthusiastically.
    A. were expecting
    B. was expecting
    C. is expected
    D. has been expecting

47. The requirements for admission to the Lettermen's Club _____ posted outside the athletic director's office for months.
    A. was   B. was being   C. has been   D. have been

48. Please give me a list of the people _____ to compete in the kayak race.
    A. whom you think have planned
    B. who you think has planned
    C. who you think is planning
    D. who you think are planning

49. I saw Eloise and Abelard earlier today; _____ were riding around in a fancy 1956 MG.
    A. she and him   B. her and him   C. she and he   D. her and he

50. If you _____ the trunk in the attic, I'll unpack it later today.
    A. can sit
    B. are able to sit
    C. can set
    D. have sat

51. _____ all of the flour been used, or may I borrow three cups?
    A. Have   B. Has   C. Is   D. Could

52. In exasperation, the cycle shop's owner suggested that _____ there too long.
    A. us boys were
    B. we boys were
    C. us boys had been
    D. we boys had been

53. Idleness as well as money _____ the root of all evil.
    A. have been
    B. were to have been
    C. is
    D. are

54. Only the string players from the quartet—Gregory, Isaac, _____—remained after the concert to answer questions.
    A. him, and I
    B. he, and I
    C. him, and me
    D. he, and me

55. Of all the antiques that _____ for sale, Gertrude chose to buy a stupid glass thimble.
    A. was
    B. is
    C. would have
    D. were

56. The detective snapped, "Don't confuse me with theories about _____ you believe committed the crime!"
    A. who   B. whom   C. whomever   D. which

57. _____ when we first called, we might have avoided our present predicament.
    A. The plumber's coming
    B. If the plumber would have come
    C. If the plumber had come
    D. If the plumber was to have come

58. We thought the sun _____ in the north until we discovered that our compass was defective.
    A. had rose
    B. had risen
    C. had rised
    D. had raised

59. Each play of Shakespeare's _____ more than _____ share of memorable characters.
    A. contain its
    B. contains; its
    C. contains; it's
    D. contain; their

60. Our English teacher suggested to _____ seniors that either Tolstoy or Dickens _____ the outstanding novelist of the nineteenth century.
    A. we; was considered
    B. we; were considered
    C. us; was considered
    D. us; were considered

61. Sherlock Holmes, together with his great friend and companion Dr. Watson, _____ to aid the woman _____ had stumbled into the room.
    A. has agreed; who
    B. have agreed; whom
    C. has agreed; whom
    D. have agreed; who

62. Several of the deer _____ when they spotted my backpack _____ open in the meadow.
    A. was frightened; laying
    B. were frightened; lying
    C. were frightened; laying
    D. was frightened; lying

63. After the Scholarship Committee announces _____ selection, hysterics often _____.
    A. it's; occur
    B. its; occur
    C. their; occur
    D. their; occurs

64. I _____ the key on the table last night so you and _____ could find it.
    A. layed; her
    B. lay; she
    C. laid; she
    D. laid; her

65. Some of the antelope _____ wandered away from the meadow where the rancher _____ the block of salt.
    A. has; sat
    B. has; set
    C. have; had set
    D. has; sets

66. Macaroni and cheese _____ best to us (that is, to Andy and _____) when Mother adds extra cheddar cheese.
    A. tastes; I
    B. tastes; me
    C. taste; me
    D. taste; I

66._____

67. Frank said, "It must have been _____ called the phone company."
    A. she who
    B. she whom
    C. her who
    D. her whom

67._____

68. The herd _____ moving restlessly at every bolt of lightning; it was either Ted or _____ who saw the beginning of the stampede.
    A. was; me
    B. were; I
    C. was; I
    D. have been; me

68._____

69. The foreman _____ his lateness by saying that his alarm clock _____ until six minutes before eight.
    A. explains; had not rang
    B. explained; has not rung
    C. has explained; rung
    D. explained; hadn't rung

69._____

70. Of all the coaches, Ms. Cox is the only one who _____ that Sherry dives more gracefully than _____.
    A. is always saying; I
    B. is always saying; me
    C. are always saying; I
    D. were always saying; me

70._____

Questions 71-90.

DIRECTIONS: Choose the word in Questions 71 through 90 that is MOST opposite in meaning to the italicized word.

71. *fact*
    A. statistic
    B. statement
    C. incredible
    D. conjecture

71._____

72. *stiff*
    A. fastidious
    B. babble
    C. supple
    D. apprehensive

72._____

73. *blunt*
    A. concise   B. tactful   C. artistic   D. humble

73._____

74. *foreign*
    A. pertinent   B. comely   C. strange   D. scrupulous

74._____

75. *anger*
    A. infer   B. pacify   C. taint   D. revile

75._____

76. *frank*
    A. earnest   B. reticent   C. post   D. expensive

76._____

77. *secure*
    A. precarious   B. acquire   C. moderate   D. frenzied

78. *petty*
    A. harmonious
    C. forthright
    B. careful
    D. momentous

79. *concede*
    A. dispute
    C. subvert
    B. reciprocate
    D. propagate

80. *benefit*
    A. liquidation
    C. detriment
    B. bazaar
    D. profit

81. *capricious*
    A. preposterous
    C. diabolical
    B. constant
    D. careless

82. *boisterous*
    A. devious   B. valiant   C. girlish   D. taciturn

83. *harmony*
    A. congruence   B. discord   C. chagrin   D. melody

84. *laudable*
    A. auspicious
    C. acclaimed
    B. despicable
    D. doubtful

85. *adherent*
    A. partisan   B. stoic   C. renegade   D. recluse

86. *exuberant*
    A. frail   B. corpulent   C. austere   D. bigot

87. *spurn*
    A. accede   B. flail   C. efface   D. annihilate

88. *spontaneous*
    A. hapless
    C. intentional
    B. corrosive
    D. willful

89. *disparage*
    A. abolish   B. exude   C. incriminate   D. extol

90. *timorous*
    A. succinct   B. chaste   C. audacious   D. insouciant

KEY (CORRECT ANSWERS)

1. D	21. A	41. A	61. A	81. B
2. C	22. B	42. D	62.	82. D
3. B	23. C	43. C	63. B	83. B
4. C	24. B	44. B	64. C	84. B
5. C	25. C	45. A	65. C	85. C
6. C	26. C	46. A	66. B	86. C
7. B	27. D	47. D	67. A	87. A
8. B	28. B	48. A	68. C	88. C
9. A	29. B	49. C	69. D	89. D
10. C	30. C	50. C	70. A	90. C
11. C	31. A	51. B	71. D	
12. D	32. B	52. D	72. C	
13. C	33. B	53. C	73. B	
14. C	34. D	54. B	74. A	
15. A	35. A	55. D	75. B	
16. C	36. B	56. B	76. B	
17. A	37. B	57. C	77. A	
18. D	38. D	58. B	78. D	
19. B	39. D	59. B	79. A	
20. B	40. A	60. C	80. C	

ENGLISH GRAMMAR AND USAGE
EXAMINATION SECTION
TEST 1

DIRECTIONS: In the passages that follow, certain words and phrases are underlined and numbered. In each question, you will find alternatives for each underlined part. You are to choose the one that BEST expresses the idea, makes the statement appropriate for standard written English, or is worded MOST consistently with the style and tone of the passage as a whole. Choose the alternative you consider BEST and write the letter in the space at the right. If you think the original version is BEST, choose NO CHANGE. Read each passage through once before you begin to answer the questions that accompany it. You cannot determine most answers without reading several sentences beyond the phrase in question. Be sure that you have read far enough ahead each time you choose an alternative.

Questions 1-14.

DIRECTIONS: Questions 1 through 14 are based on the following passage.

Modern filmmaking <u>had began</u> in Paris in 1895 with the work of the Lumiere brothers.
                        1
Using their <u>invention, the Cinématographe,</u> the Lumières were able to photograph, print,
            2
and project moving pictures onto a screen. Their films showed <u>actual occurrences. A</u> train
                                                                           3
approaching a station, people a factory, workers demolishing a wall.

These early films had neither plot nor sound. But another Frenchman, Georges Méliès,
soon incorporated plot lines <u>into</u> his films. And with his attempts to draw upon the potential of
                              4
film to create fantasy <u>worlds.</u> Méliès also <u>was an early pioneer from</u> special film effects. Edwin
                        5   6
Porter, an American filmmaker, took Méliès emphasis on narrative one step further. Believing
<u>that, continuity of shots</u> was of primary importance in filmmaking, Porter connected
      7
<u>images to present,</u> a sustained action. His GREAT TRAIN ROBBERY of 1903 opened a new
      8
era in film.

<u>Because</u> film was still considered <u>as</u> *low* entertainment in early twentieth century America,
    9   10
it was on its way to becoming a respected art form. Beginning in 1908, the American director

D.W. Griffith discovered and explored techniques to make film a more expressive medium.

2 (#1)

With his technical contributions, as well as his attempts to develop the intellectual and moral
                              11
potential of film, Griffith helped build a solid foundation for the industry.

   Thirty years after the Lumière brothers' first show, sound had yet been added to the
    12   13
movies. Finally, in 1927, Hollywood produced its first *talkie*, THE JAZZ SINGER. With sound,

modern film coming of age.
              14

1. A. NO CHANGE   B. begun   1.____
    C. began   D. had some beginnings

2. A. NO CHANGE   B. invention—the Cinématographe   2.____
    C. invention, the Cinématgraphe— D. invention, the Cinématographe

3. A. NO CHANGE   B. actually occurrences, a   3.____
    C. actually occurrences—a   D. actual occurrences: a

4. A. NO CHANGE   B. about   4.____
    C. with   D. to

5. A. NO CHANGE   B. worlds   5.____
    C. worlds' and   D. worlds and

6. A. NO CHANGE   B. pioneered   6.____
    C. pioneered the beginnings of   D. pioneered the early beginnings of

7. A. NO CHANGE   B. that continuity of shots   7.____
    C. that, continuity of shots,   D. that continuity of shots

8. A. NO CHANGE   B. images to present   8.____
    C. that, continuity of shots   D. that continuity of shots

9. A. NO CHANGE   9.____
    B. (Begin new paragraph) in view of the fact that
    C. (Begin new paragraph) Although
    D. Do NOT begin new paragraph) Since

10. A. NO CHANGE   B. as if it were   10.____
    C. like it was   D. OMIT the underlined portion

11. A. NO CHANGE   B. similar to   11.____
    C. similar with   D. like with

86

3 (#1)

12. A. NO CHANGE
    B. (Begin new paragraph) Consequently, thirty
    C. (Do NOT begin new paragraph) Therefore, thirty
    D. (Do NOT begin new paragraph) As a consequence, thirty

12._____

13. A. NO CHANGE
    B. (Begin new paragraph) Consequently, thirty
    C. (No NOT begin new paragraph) Therefore, thirty
    D. (Do NOT begin new paragraph As a consequence, thirty

13._____

14. A. NO CHANGE   B. comes
    C. came   D. had came

14._____

Questions 15-22.

DIRECTIONS: Questions 15 through 22 are based on the following passage.

One of the most awesome forces in nature is the tsunami, or tidal wave. A

<u>tsunami—the word is Japanese for harbor wave,</u> can generate the destructive power of many
                15

atomic bombs.

    <u>Tsunamis usually</u> appear in a series of four or five waves about fifteen minutes apart.
        16

They begin deep in the ocean, gather remarkable speed as they travel, and cover great

instances. The wave triggered by the explosion of Krakatoa in 1883 circled the world in three

days.

    <u>Tsunamis being</u> known to sink large ships at sea, they are most dangerous when they
       17

reach land. Close to shore, an oncoming tsunami is forced <u>upward and skyward,</u> perhaps as
                                                             18

high as 100 feet. This combination of height and speed accounts for the tsunami's great power.

    That *tsunami* is a Japanese word is no accident, <u>due to the fact that</u> no nation
                                                                        19

<u>frequently</u> has been so visited by giant waves as Japan. <u>Tsunamis</u> reach that country regularly,
  20   21

and with devastating consequences. One Japanese tsunami flattened several towns in

<u>1896, also killed 27,000 people.</u> The 2011 tsunami caused similar loss of life as well as untold
       22

damage from nuclear radiation.

15. A. NO CHANGE
    B. tsunami, the word is Japanese for harbor wave—
    C. tsunami—the word is Japanese for harbor wave—
    D. tsunami—the word being Japanese for harbor wave,

16. A. NO CHANGE
    B. (Begin new paragraph) Consequently, tsunamis
    C. (Do NOT begin new paragraph) Tsunamis consequently
    D. (Do NOT begin new paragraph) Yet, tsunamis

17. A. NO CHANGE   B. Because tsunamis have been
    C. Although tsunamis have been   D. Tsunamis have been

18. A. NO CHANGE   B. upward to the sky,
    C. upward in the sky   D. upward,

19. A. NO CHANGE
    B. when one takes into consideration the fact that
    C. seeing as how
    D. for

20. A. NO CHANGE   B. (Place after *has*)
    C. (Place after *so*)   D. (Place after *visited*)

21. A. NO CHANGE   B. Moreover, tsunamis
    C. However, tsunamis   D. Because tsunamis

22. A. NO CHANGE   B. 1896 and killed 27,000 people
    C. 1896 and killing 27,000 people   D. 1896, and 27,000 people as well

Questions 23-33.

DIRECTIONS: Questions 23 through 33 are based on the following passage.

I was <u>married one</u> August on a farm in Maine. The <u>ceremony, itself, taking</u> place in an
         23   24
arbor of pine boughs <u>we had built and constructed</u> in the yard next to the house. On the morning
                     25
of the wedding day, we parked the tractors behind the shed, <u>have tied</u> the dogs to an oak tree to
                                                              26
keep them from chasing the guests, and put the cows out to pasture. <u>Thus</u> we had thought of
                                                                     27
everything, it seemed. we had forgotten how interested a cow can be in what is going on

<u>around them.</u> During the ceremony, my sister <u>(who has taken several years of lessons)</u> was to
   28   29
play a flute solo. We were all listening intently when she <u>had began</u> to play. As the first notes
                                                            30
reached us, we were surprised to hear a bass line under the flute's treble melody. Looking

around, the source was quickly discovered. There was Star, my pet Guernsey, her head hanging
                   31
over the pasture fence, mooing along with the delicate strains of Bach.

Star took our laughter as being like a compliment, and we took her contribution that way,
                              32
too. It was a sign of approval—the kind you would find only at a farm wedding.

23. A. NO CHANGE B. married, one 23.____
    C. married on an D. married, in an

24. A. NO CHANGE B. ceremony itself taking 24.____
    C. ceremony itself took D. ceremony, itself took

25. A. NO CHANGE 25.____
    B. which had been built and constructed
    C. we had built and constructed it
    D. we had built

26. A. NO CHANGE B. tie 26.____
    C. tied D. tying

27. A. NO CHANGE 27.____
    B. (Do NOT begin new paragraph) And
    C. (Begin new paragraph) But
    D. (Begin new paragraph (Moreover,

28. A. NO CHANGE B. around her 28.____
    C. in her own vicinity D. in their immediate area

29. A. NO CHANGE 29.____
    B. (whom has taken many years of lessons)
    C. (who has been trained in music)
    D. OMIT the underlined portion

30. A. NO CHANGE B. begun 30.____
    C. began D. would begin

31. A. NO CHANGE 31.____
    B. the discovery of the source was quick
    C. the discovery of the source was quickly made.
    D. we quickly discovered the source.

32. A. NO CHANGE A. as 32.____
    C. just as D. as if

33. A. NO CHANGE B. Yet it was
    C. But it was D. Being

Questions 34-42.

DIRECTIONS: Questions 34 through 42 are based on the following passage,

Riding a bicycle in Great Britain is not the same as riding a bicycle in the United States. Americans bicycling in Britain will find some <u>basic fundamental</u> differences in the rules of the
34
road and in the attitudes of motorists.

<u>Probably</u> most difficult for the American cyclist is adjusting <u>with</u> British traffic patterns.
35 36
<u>Knowing that traffic</u> in Britain moves on the left-hand side of the road, bicycling <u>once</u> there is the
37 38
mirror image of what it is in the United States.

The problem of adjusting to traffic patterns is somewhat lessened, <u>however</u> by the respect
39
with which British motorists treat bicyclists. A cyclist in a traffic circle, for example, is given the same right-of-way <u>with</u> the driver of any other vehicle. However, the cyclist is expected to obey
40
the rules of the road. <u>This difference in the American and British attitudes toward bicyclists</u> may
41
stem from differing attitudes toward the bicycle itself. Whereas Americans frequently view bicycles as <u>toys, but</u> the British treat them primarily as vehicles.
42

34. A. NO CHANGE   B. basic and fundamental
    C. basically fundamental D. basic

35. A. NO CHANGE   B. Even so, probably
    C. Therefore, probably D. As a result, probably

36. A. NO CHANGE   B. upon
    C. on   D. to

37. A. NO CHANGE   B. Seeing that traffic
    C. Because traffic   D. Traffic

38. A. NO CHANGE   B. once you are
    C. once one is   D. OMIT the underlined portion

7 (#1)

39. A. NO CHANGE   B. also,   39.____
    C. moreover,   D. therefore,

40. A. NO CHANGE   B. as   40.____
    C. as if   D. as with

41. A. NO CHANGE   41.____
    B. difference in the American and British attitudes toward bicyclists
    C. difference, in the American and British attitudes toward bicyclists
    D. difference in the American, and British, attitudes toward bicyclists

42. A. NO CHANGE   B. toy;   42.____
    C. toys,   D. toys; but

Questions 43-51.

DIRECTIONS: Questions 43 through 51 are based on the following passage.

People have always believed that supernatural powers <u>tend toward some influence on</u> lives for good or for ill. Superstition originated with the idea that individuals <u>could in turn,</u> exert
                                                             43   44

influence <u>at</u> spirits. Certain superstitions are <u>so deeply embedded</u> in our culture that intelligent
         45   46
people sometimes act in accordance with them.

One common superstitious act is knocking on wood after boasting of good fortune. People once believed that gods inhabited trees and, therefore, were present in the wood used to build houses. Fearing that speaking of good luck within the gods' hearing might anger <u>them, people</u>
                                                                                          47
knocked on wood to deafen the gods and avoid their displeasure.

Another superstitious <u>custom and practice</u> is throwing salt over the left shoulder.
                                         48
<u>Considering</u> salt was once considered sacred, people thought that spilling it brought bad
  49
luck. Since right and left represented good and evil, the believers used their right hands, which symbolized good, to throw a pinch of salt over their left shoulders into the eyes of the evil gods. <u>Because of this</u>, people attempted to avert misfortune.
    50
Without realizing the origin of superstitions, many people exhibit superstitious behavior.

<u>Others avoid</u> walking under ladders and stepping on cracks in sidewalks, without having any
    51
idea why they are doing so.

91

43. A. NO CHANGE
    C. tend to influence on
    C. can influence
    D. are having some influence on

44. A. NO CHANGE.
    C. could, in turn
    B. could, turning
    D. could, in turn,

45. A. NO CHANGE
    C. toward
    C. of
    D. on

46. A. NO CHANGE
    C. deepest embedded
    B. deepest embedded
    D. embedded deepest

47. A. NO CHANGE
    C. them: some people
    B. them; some people
    D. them, they

48. A. NO CHANGE
    C traditional custom
    B. Custom
    D. customary habit

49. A. NO CHANGE
    C. Because
    B. Although
    D. Keeping in mind that

50. A. NO CHANGE
    C. Consequently
    B. As a result of this,
    D. In this way,

51. A. NO CHANGE
    C. Avoiding
    B. Often avoiding
    D. They avoid

Questions 52-66.

DIRECTIONS: Questions 52 through 65 are based on the following passage.

In the 1920s, the Y.M.C.A. sponsored one of the first programs <u>in order to promote</u>
                                                                        52
more enlightened public opinion on racial matters; the organization started special university

classes <u>in which</u> young people could study race relations. Among the guest speakers invited to
         53
conduct the sessions, one of the most popular was George Washington Carver, the scientist

from Tuskegee Institute.

As a student, Carver himself had been active in the Y.M.C.A. <u>He shared</u> its evangelical
                                                                    54
and educational philosophy. However, in <u>1923,</u> the Y.M.C.A. arranged <u>Carver's first initial</u>
                                          55   56
speaking tour, the scientist accepted with apprehension. He was to speak at several white

colleges, most of whose students had never seen, let alone heard, an educated black man.

9 (#1)

Although Carver's appearances did sometimes cause occasional controversy, but
                                  57   58
his quiet dedication prevailed, and his humor quickly won over his audiences. Nevertheless, for
                                                                                59
the next decade, Carver toured the Northeast, Midwest, and South under Y.M.C.A.

sponsorship. Speaking at places never before open to blacks. On these tours Carver
              60
befriended thousands of students, many of whom subsequently corresponded with his
                                              61
afterwards. The tours, unfortunately were not without discomfort for Carver. There were
    62   63
the indignities of *Jim Crow* accommodations and racial insults from strangers. As a result,
                                                                                 64
the scientist's enthusiasm never faltered. Avoiding any discussion of the political and social
                                           65
aspects of racial injustice; instead, Carver conducted his whole life as an indirect attack to
                                                                                          66
prejudice. This, as much as his science, is his legacy to humankind.

52. A. NO CHANGE   B. to promote   52.____
    C. for the promoting of what is   D. for the promotion of what are

53. A. NO CHANGE   C. from which   53.____
    C. that   D. by which

54. A. NO CHANGE   B. Sharing.   54.____
    C. Having Shared   D. Because He Shared

55. A. NO CHANGE   B. 1923   55.____
    C. 1923, and   D. 1923, when

56. A. NO CHANGE   B. Carvers' first, initial   56.____
    C. Carvers first initial   D. Carver's first

57. A. NO CHANGE   B. sometimes did   57.____
    C. did   D. OMIT the underlined portion

58. A. NO CHANGE   B. controversy and   58.____
    C. controversy   D. controversy, however

59. A. NO CHANGE   B. However, for   59.____
    C. However, from   D. For

60. A. NO CHANGE   B. sponsorship and spoke   60.____
    C. sponsorship; and spoke   D. sponsorship, and speaking

93

61. A. NO CHANGE B. who
    C. them D. those 61.____

62. A. NO CHANGE 62.____
    B. later
    C. sometimes later.
    D. OMIT the underlined portion and end the sentence with a period

63. A. NO CHANGE B. tours, unfortunately, were 63.____
    C. tours unfortunately, were D. tours, unfortunately, are

64. A. NO CHANGE B. So 64.____
    C. But D. Therefore,

65. A. NO CHANGE B. He avoided discussing 65.____
    C. Having avoided discussing D. Upon avoiding the discussion of

66. A. NO CHANGE B. over 66.____
    C. on D. of

Questions 67-75.

DIRECTIONS: Questions 67 through 75 are based on the following passage.

　　Shooting rapids is not the only way to experience the thrill of canoeing. <u>An ordinary-</u>
　　　　　　　　　　　　　　　　　　　　　　　　　　　　　　　　　　　　　　　67
looking stream, innocent of rocks and white water, can provide adventure, as long as it has

three essential <u>features</u>; a swift current, close banks, and <u>has</u> plenty of twists and turns.
　　　　　　　　　68　　　　　　　　　　　　　　　　　　　　　　　　69

<u>A</u> powerful current causes tension, for canoeists know they will have only seconds for
70
executing the maneuvers necessary to prevent crashing into the threes lining the narrow

<u>streams banks</u>. Of course, the <u>narrowness, itself, being</u> crucial in creating the tension. On a
　　　71　　　　　　　　　　　　　　　　　72
broad stream, canoeists can pause frequently, catch their breath, and get their bearings.

However <u>to</u> a narrow stream, where every minute <u>you run</u> the risk of being knocked down by a
　　　　　　73　　　　　　　　　　　　　　　　　74
low-hanging tree limb, they be constantly alert. Yet even the fast current and close banks would

be manageable if the stream were fairly straight. The expenditure of energy required to paddle

furiously, first on one side of the canoe and then on the other, wearies <u>both the nerves as well</u>
　　75
as the body.

94

11 (#1)

67.
- A. NO CHANGE
- B. They say that for adventure an
- C. Many finding that an
- D. The old saying that an

67._____

68.
- A. NO CHANGE
- B. features
- C. features,
- D. features; these being

68._____

69.
- A. NO CHANGE
- B. there must be
- C. with
- D. OMIT the underlined portion

69._____

70.
- A. NO CHANGE
- B. Thus, a
- C. Therefore, a
- D. Furthermore, a

70._____

71.
- A. NO CHANGE
- B. stream's banks.
- C. streams bank's
- D. banks of the streams

71._____

72.
- A. NO CHANGE
- B. narrowness, itself is
- C. narrowness itself is
- D. narrowness in itself being

72._____

73.
- A. NO CHANGE
- B. near
- C. on
- D. with

73._____

74.
- A. NO CHANGE
- B. the canoer runs
- C. one runs
- D. they run

74._____

75.
- A. NO CHANGE
- B. the nerves as well as the body
- C. the nerves, also, as well as the body
- D. not only the body but also the nerves as well

75._____

KEY (CORRECT ANSWERS)

1.	C	21.	A	41.	A	61.	A
2.	A	22.	B	42.	C	62.	D
3.	D	23.	A	43.	B	63.	B
4.	A	24.	C	44.	C	64.	C
5.	B	25.	D	45.	D	65.	B
6.	B	26.	C	46.	A	66.	C
7.	D	27.	C	47.	A	67.	A
8.	B	28.	B	48.	B	68.	B
9.	C	29.	D	49.	C	69.	D
10.	D	30.	C	50.	D	70.	A
11.	A	31.	D	51.	D	71.	B
12.	A	32.	B	52.	B	72.	C
13.	B	33.	A	53.	A	73.	C
14.	C	34.	D	54.	A	74.	D
15.	C	35.	A	55.	D	75.	B
16.	A	36.	D	56.	D		
17.	C	37.	C	57.	C		
18.	D	38.	D	58.	C		
19.	D	39.	A	59.	D		
20.	C	40.	B	60.	B		

EXAMINATION SECTION
TEST 1

DIRECTIONS: Each question or incomplete statement is followed by several suggested answers or completions. Select the one that BEST answers the question or completes the statement. *PRINT THE LETTER OF THE CORRECT ANSWER IN THE SPACE AT THE RIGHT.*

Questions 1-25. A student has written an article for the high school newspaper, using the skills learned in a stenography and typewriting class in its preparation. In the article which follows, certain words or groups of words are underlined and numbered. The underlined word or group of words may be incorrect because they present an error in grammar, usage, sentence structure, capitalization, diction, or punctuation. For each numbered word or group of words, there is an identically numbered question consisting of four choices based only on the underlined portion. Indicate the BEST choice. <u>Unnecessary changes will be considered incorrect.</u>

TIGERS VIE FOR CITY CHAMPIONSHIP

In their second year of varsity football, the North Shore Tigers have gained a shot at the city championship. Last Saturday in the play-offs, the Tigers defeated the Western High School Cowboys, <u>thus eliminated that team</u> from contention. Most of the credit for the
(1)
team's improvement must go to Joe Harris, the coach. <u>To play as well as they do</u> now,
(2)
the coach must have given the team superior instruction. There is no doubt that,

<u>if a coach is effective, his influence is over</u> many young minds.
(3)
With this major victory behind them, the Tigers can now look forward <u>to meet the</u>
(4)
defending champions, the Revere Minutemen, in the finals.

The win over the Cowboys was <u>due</u> to North Side's supremacy in the air. The Tigers'
(5)
players have the advantages of strength and of <u>being speedy</u>. Our sterling quarterback, Butch
(6)
Carter, a master of the long pass, used <u>these kind of passes</u> to bedevil the boys from Western.
(7)
As a matter of fact, if the Tigers <u>would have used</u> the passing offense earlier in the game, the
(8)
score would have been more one-sided. Butch, by the way, our all-around senior student, has already been tapped for bigger things. Having the highest marks in his class, <u>Barton College</u>

2 (#1)

has offered him a scholarship.
       (9)

The team's defense is another story. During the last few weeks, neither the linebackers nor the safety man have shown sufficient ability to contain their opponents' running game. In
                                                                (10)
the city final, the defensive unit's failing to complete it's assignments may lead to disaster.
                (11)
However, the coach said that this unit not only has been cooperative but also the coach raise
                                           (12)
their eagerness to learn. He also said that this team has not and never will give up. This kind
                                                              (13)
of spirit is contagious, therefore I predict that the Tigers will win because I have affection and full
                          (14)   (15)
confidence in the team.

One of the happy surprises this season is Peter Yisko, our punter. Peter is in the United
                                                                                        (16)
States for only two years. When he was in grammar school in the old country, it was not necessary for him to have studied hard. Now, he depends on the football team to help him with
                        (17)
his English. Everybody but the team mascot and I have been pressed into service. Peter was
                         (18)
ineligible last year when he learned that he would only obtain half of the credits he had
                                 (19)
completed in Europe. Nevertheless, he attended occasional practice sessions, but he soon found out that, if one wants to be a successful player, you must realize that regular practice is
                                                                 (20)
required. In fact, if a team is to be successful, it is necessary that everyone be present for all
                                                                                   (21)
practice sessions. "The life of a football player," says Peter, "is better than a scholar."
                                                                                  (22)
Facing the Minutemen, the Tigers will meet their most formidable opposition yet. This team is not only gaining a bad reputation but also indulging in illegal practices on the field.
        (23)
They can't hardly object to us being technical about penalties under these circumstances.
      (24)
As far as the Minutemen are concerned, a victory will taste sweet like a victory should.
                                            (25)

1. A. that eliminated that team   B. and they were eliminated   1._____
    C. and eliminated them   D. Correct as is

98

3 (#1)

2. A. To make them play as well as they do
   B. Having played so well
   C. After they played so well
   D. Correct as is

   2.____

3. A. if coaches are effective; they have influence over
   B. to be effective, a coach influences over
   C. if a coach is effective, he influences
   D. Correct as is

   3.____

4. A. to meet with   B. to meeting
   C. to a meeting of   D. Correct as is

   4.____

5. A. because of   B. on account of
   C. motivated by   D. Correct as is

   5.____

6. A. operating swiftly   B. speed
   C. running speedily   D. Correct as is

   6.____

7. A. these kinds of pass   B. this kind of passes
   C. this kind of pass   D. Correct as is

   7.____

8. A. would of used   B. had used
   C. were using   D. Correct as is

   8.____

9. A. he was offered a scholarship by Barton College.
   B. Barton College offered a scholarship to him.
   C. a scholarship was offered him by Barton College
   D. Correct as is

   9.____

10. A. had shown   B. were showing
    C. has shown   D. Correct as is

    10.____

11. A. the defensive unit failing to complete its assignment
    B. the defensive unit's failing to complete its assignment
    C. the defensive unit failing to complete it's assignment
    D. Correct as is

    11.____

12. A. has been not only cooperative, but also eager to learn
    B. has not only been cooperative, but also shows eagerness to learn
    C. has been not only cooperative, but also they were eager to learn
    D. Correct as is

    12.____

13. A. has not given up and never will
    B. has not and never would give up
    C. has not given up and never will give up
    D. Correct as is

    13.____

14. A. .Therefore B. : therefore 14.____
    C. —therefore D. Correct as is

15. A. full confidence and affection for 15.____
    B. affection for and full confidence in
    C. affection and full confidence concerning
    D. Correct as is

16. A. is living B. was living 16.____
    C. has been D. Correct as is

17. A. to study B. to be studying 17.____
    C. to have been studying D. Correct as is

18. A. but the team mascot and me has 18.____
    B. but the team mascot and myself has
    C. but the team mascot and me have
    D. Correct as is

19. A. only learned that he would obtain half 19.____
    B. learned that he would obtain only half
    C. learned that he only would obtain half
    D. Correct as is

20. A. a person B. one 20.____
    C. one D. every

21. A. is B. will be 21.____
    C. shall be D. Correct as is

22. A. to be a scholar B. being a scholar 22.____
    C. that of a scholar D. Correct as is

23. A. not only is gaining a bad reputation 23.____
    B. is gaining not only a bad reputation
    C. is not gaining only a bad reputation
    D. Correct as is

24. A. can hardly object to us being B. can hardly object to our being 24.____
    C. can't hardly object to our being D. Correct as is

25. A victory will taste sweet like it should 25.____
    B. victory will taste sweetly as it should taste
    C. victory will taste sweet as a victory should
    D. Correct as is

Questions 26-30.

DIRECTIONS: Questions 26 through 30 are to be answered on the basis of the instructions and paragraph which follow.

The paragraph which follows is part of report prepared by a buyer for submission to his superior. The paragraph contains 5 underlined groups of words, each one bearing a number which identifies the question relating to it. Each of these groups of words MAY or MAY NOT represent standard written English, suitable for use in a formal report. For each question, decide whether the group of words used in the paragraph which is always choice A is standard written English and should be retained, or whether choice B, C, or D.

On October 23, 2009 the vendor delivered two microscopes to the using agency. <u>When they inspected</u>, one microscope was found to have a defective part. The vendor was
     (26)
notified, and offered to replace the defective part; the using agency, however, requested <u>that the microscope be replaced</u>. The vendor claimed that complete replacement was
     (27)
unnecessary and refused to comply with the agency's demand, <u>having the result that the
                                                                                                      (28)
agency declared</u> that it will pay only for the acceptable microscope. At that point <u>I got involved by the agency's contacting me. The agency requested that I speak to the vendor
                                         (29)
since I handled the original purchase and have dealt with this vendor before.</u>
                                                                                                    (30)

26. A. When they inspected
    B. Upon inspection
    C. The inspection report said that
    D. Having inspected,

27. A. that the microscope be replaced
    B. a whole new microscope in replacement
    C. to have a replacement for the microscope
    D. that they get the microscope replaced

28. A. , having the result that the agency declared
    B. ; the agency consequently declared
    C. , which refusal caused the agency to consequently declare
    D. , with the result of the agency's declaring

29. A. I got involved by the agency's contacting me
    B. I became involved, being contacted by the agency
    C. the agency contacting me, I got involved
    D. the agency contacted me and I became involved

30. A. have dealed with this vendor before.
    B. done business before with this vendor.
    C. know this vendor by prior dealings
    D. have dealt with this vendor before.

30.____

KEY (CORRECT ANSWERS)

1.	C	11.	B	21.	D
2.	A	12.	A	22.	C
3.	C	13.	B	23.	D
4.	B	14.	A	24.	A
5.	A	15.	B	25.	C
6.	B	16.	C	26.	B
7.	C	17.	A	27.	A
8.	B	18.	A	28.	B
9.	D	19.	B	29.	D
10.	C	20.	C	30.	D

EXAMINATION SECTION
TEST 1

DIRECTIONS: In each of the following questions, only one of the four sentences conforms to standards of correct usage. The other three contain errors in grammar, diction, or punctuation. Select the choice in each question which BEST conforms to standards of correct usage. Consider a choice correct if it contains none of the errors mentioned above, even though there may be other ways of expressing the same thought. *PRINT THE LETTER OF THE CORRECT ANSWER IN THE SPACE AT THE RIGHT.*

1. A. Because he was ill was no excuse for his behavior
   B. I insist that he see a lawyer before he goes to trial.
   C. He said "that he had not intended to go."
   D. He wasn't out of the office only three days.

   1.____

2. A. He came to the station and pays a porter to carry his bags into the train.
   B. I should have liked to live in medieval times.
   C. My father was born in Linville. A little country town where everybody knows everyone else.
   D. The car, which is parked across the street, is disabled.

   2.____

3. A. He asked the desk clerk for a clean, quiet, room.
   B. I expected James to be lonesome and that he would want to go home.
   C. I have stopped worrying because I have heard nothing further on the subject.
   D. If the board of directors controls the company, they may take actions which are disapproved by the stockholders.

   3.____

4. A. Each of the players knew their place.
   B. He whom you saw on the stage is the son of an actor.
   C. Susan is the smartest of the twin sisters.
   D. Who ever thought of him winning both prizes?

   4.____

5. A. An outstanding trait of early man was their reliance on omens.
   B. Because I had never been there before.
   C. Neither Mr. Jones nor Mr. Smith has completed his work.
   D. While eating my dinner, a dog came to the window.

   5.____

6. A. A copy of the lease, in addition to the Rules and Regulations, are to be given to each tenant.
   B. The Rules and Regulations and a copy of the lease is being given to each tenant.
   C. A copy of the lease, in addition to the Rules and Regulations, is to be given to each tenant.
   D. A copy of the lease, in addition to the Rules and Regulations, are being given to each tenant.

   6.____

2 (#1)

7. A. Although we understood that for him music was a passion, we were disturbed by the fact that he was addicted to sing along with the soloists.
    B. Do you believe that Steven is liable to win a scholarship?
    C. Give the picture to whomever is a connoisseur of art.
    D. Whom do you believe to be the most efficient worker in the office?

    7.____

8. A. Each adult who is sure they know all the answers will some day realize their mistake.
    B. Even the most hardhearted villain would have to feel bad about so horrible a tragedy.
    C. Neither being licensed teachers, both aspirants had to pass rigorous tests before being appointed.
    D. The principal reason why he wanted to be designated was because he had never before been to a convention.

    8.____

9. A. Being that the weather was so inclement, the party has been postponed for at least a month.
    B. He is in New York City only three weeks and he has already seen all the thrilling sights in Manhattan and in the other four boroughs.
    C. If you will look it up in the official directory, which can be consulted in the library during specified hours, you will discover that the chairman and director are Mr. T. Henry Long.
    D. Working hard at college during the day and at the post office during the night, he appeared to his family to be indefatigable.

    9.____

10. A. I would have been happy to oblige you if you only asked me to do it.
    B. The cold weather, as well as the unceasing wind and rain, have made us decide to spend the winter in Florida.
    C. The politician would have been more successful in winning office if he would have been less dogmatic.
    D. These trousers are expensive; however, they will wear well.

    10.____

11. A. All except him wore formal attire at the reception for the ambassador.
    B. If that chair were to be blown off of the balcony, it might injure someone below.
    C. Not a passenger, who was in the crash, survived the impact.
    D. To borrow money off friends is the best way to lose them.

    11.____

12. A. Approaching Manhattan on the ferry boat from Staten Island, an unforgettable sight of the skyscrapers is seen.
    B. Did you see the exhibit of modernistic paintings as yet?
    C. Gesticulating wildly and ranting in stentorian tones, the speaker was the sinecure of all eyes.
    D. The airplane with crew and passengers was lost somewhere in the Pacific Ocean.

    12.____

13. A. If one has consistently had that kind of training, it is certainly too late to change your entire method of swimming long distances.
    B. The captain would have been more impressed if you would have been more conscientious in evacuation drills.
    C. The passengers on the stricken ship were all ready to abandon it at the signal.
    D. The villainous shark lashed at the lifeboat with it's tail, trying to upset the rocking boat in order to partake of it's contents.

13._____

14. A. As one whose been certified as a professional engineer, I believe that the decision to build a bridge over that harbor is unsound.
    B. Between you and me, this project ought to be completed long before winter arrives.
    C. He fervently hoped that the men would be back at camp and to find them busy at their usual chores.
    D. Much to his surprise, he discovered that the climate of Korea was like his home town.

14._____

15. A. An industrious executive is aided, not impeded, by having a hobby which gives him a fresh point of view on life and its problems.
    B. Frequent absence during the calendar year will surely mitigate against the chances of promotion.
    C. He was unable to go to the committee meeting because he was very ill.
    D. Mr. Brown expressed his disapproval so emphatically that his associates were embarassed

15._____

16. A. At our next session, the office manager will have told you something about his duties and responsibilities.
    B. In general, the book is absorbing and original and have no hesitation about recommending it.
    C. The procedures followed by private industry in dealing with lateness and absence are different from ours.
    D. We shall treat confidentially any information about Mr. Doe, to whom we understand you have sent reports to for many years.

16._____

17. A. I talked to one official, whom I knew was fully impartial.
    B. Everyone signed the petition but him.
    C. He proved not only to be a good student but also a good athlete.
    D. All are incorrect.

17._____

18. A. Every year a large amount of tenants are admitted to housing projects.
    B. Henry Ford owned around a billion dollars in industrial equipment.
    C. He was aggravated by the child's poor behavior.
    D. All are incorrect.

18._____

19. A. Before he was committed to the asylum he suffered from the illusion that 19.____
       he was Napoleon.
    B. Besides stocks, there were also bonds in the safe.
    C. We bet the other team easily.
    D. All are incorrect.

20. A. Bring this report to your supervisory. 20.____
    B. He set the chair down near the table.
    C. The capitol of New York is Albany.
    D. All are incorrect.

21. A. He was chosen to arbitrate the dispute because everyone knew he would 21.____
       be disinterested.
    B. It is advisable to obtain the best council before making an important
       decision.
    C. Less college students are interested in teaching than ever before.
    D. All are incorrect.

22. A. She, hearing a signal, the source lamp flashed. 22.____
    B. While hearing a signal, the source lamp flashed.
    C. In hearing a signal, the source lamp flashed.
    D. As she heard a signal, the source lamp flashed.

23. A. Every one of the time records have been initialed in the designated spaces. 23.____
    B. All of the time records has been initialed in the designated spaces.
    C. Each one of the time records was initialed in the designated spaces.
    D. The time records all been initialed in the designated spaces.

24. A. If there is no one else to answer the phone, you will have to answer it. 24.____
    B. You will have to answer it yourself if no one else answers the phone.
    C. If no one else is not around to pick up the phone, you will have to do it.
    D. You will have to answer the phone when nobodys here to do it.

25. A. Dr. Barnes not in his office. What could I do for you? 25.____
    B. Dr. Barnes is not in his office. Is there something I can do for you?
    C. Since Dr. Barnes is not in his office, might there be something I may do for
       you?
    D. Is there any ways I can assist you since Dr. Barnes is not in his office?

26. A. She do not understand how the new console works. 26.____
    B. The way the new console works, she doesn't understand.
    C. She doesn't understand how the new console works.
    D. The new console works, so that she doesn't understand.

27. A. Certain changes in my family income must be reported as they occur. 27.____
    B. When certain changes in family income occur, it must be reported.
    C. Certain family income change must be reported as they occur.
    D. Certain changes in family income must be reported as they have been
       occurring.

28. A. Each tenant has to complete the application themselves.
    B. Each of the tenants have to complete the application by himself.
    C. Each of the tenants has to complete the application himself.
    D. Each of the tenants has to complete the application by themselves.

28._____

29. A. Yours is the only building that the construction will effect.
    B. Your's is the only building affected by the construction.
    C. The construction will only effect your building.
    D. Yours is the only building that will be affected by the construction.

29._____

30. A. There is four tests left.
    B. The number of tests left are four.
    C. There are four tests left.
    D. Four of the tests remains.

30._____

31. A. Each of the applicants takes a test.
    B. Each of the applicant take a test.
    C. Each of the applicants take tests.
    D. Each of the applicants have taken tests.

31._____

32. A. The applicant, not the examiners, are ready.
    B. The applicants, not the examiners, is ready.
    C. The applicants, not the examiner, are ready.
    D. The applicant, not the examiner, are ready

32._____

33. A. You will not progress except you practice.
    B. You will not progress without you practicing.
    C. You will not progress unless you practice.
    D. You will not progress provided you do not practice.

33._____

34. A. Neither the director or the employees will be at the office tomorrow.
    B. Neither the director nor the employees will be at the office tomorrow.
    C. Neither the director, or the secretary nor the other employees will be at the office tomorrow.
    D. Neither the director, the secretary or the other employees will be at the office tomorrow.

34._____

35. A. In my absence, he and her will have to finish the assignment.
    B. In my absence he and she will have to finish the assignment.
    C. In my absence she and him, they will have to finish the assignment.
    D. In my absence he and her both will have to finish the assignment.

35._____

KEY (CORRECT ANSWERS)

1.	B	11.	A	21.	A	31.	A
2.	B	12.	D	22.	D	32.	C
3.	C	13.	C	23.	C	33.	C
4.	B	14.	B	24.	A	34.	B
5.	C	15.	A	25.	B	35.	B
6.	C	16.	C	26.	C		
7.	D	17.	B	27.	A		
8.	B	18.	D	28.	C		
9.	D	19.	B	29.	D		
10.	D	20.	B	30.	C		

TEST 2

DIRECTIONS: Each question or incomplete statement is followed by several suggested answers or completions. Select the one that BEST answers the question or completes the statement. *PRINT THE LETTER OF THE CORRECT ANSWER IN THE SPACE AT THE RIGHT.*

Questions 1-4.

DIRECTIONS: Questions 1 through 4 consist of three sentences each. For each question, select the sentence which contains NO error in grammar or usage.

1. A. Be sure that everybody brings his notes to the conference. 1.____
   B. He looked like he meant to hit the boy.
   C. Mr. Jones is one of the clients who was chosen to represent the district.
   D. All are incorrect.

2. A. He is taller than I. 2.____
   B. I'll have nothing to do with these kind of people.
   C. The reason why he will not buy the house is because it is too expensive.
   D. All are incorrect.

3. A. Aren't I eligible for this apartment. 3.____
   B. Have you seen him anywheres?
   C. He should of come earlier.
   D. All are incorrect.

4. A. He graduated college in 2022. 4.____
   B. He hadn't but one more line to write.
   C. Who do you think is the author of this report?
   D. All are incorrect.

Questions 5-35.

DIRECTIONS: In each of the following questions, only one of the four sentences conforms to standards of correct usage. The other three contain errors in grammar, diction, or punctuation. Select the choice in each question which BEST conforms to standards of correct usage. Consider a choice correct if it contains none of the errors mentioned above, even though there may be other ways of expressing the same thought.

5. A. It is obvious that no one wants to be a kill-joy if they can help it. 5.____
   B. It is not always possible, and perhaps it never ispossible, to judge a person's character by just looking at him.
   C. When Yogi Berra of the New York Yankees hit an immortal grandslam home run, everybody in the huge stadium including Pittsburgh fans, rose to his feet.
   D. Every one of us students must pay tuition today.

6. A. The physician told the young mother that if the baby is not able to digest its milk, it should be boiled.
   B. There is no doubt whatsoever that he felt deeply hurt because John Smith had betrayed the trust.
   C. Having partaken of a most delicious repast prepared by Tessie Breen, the hostess, the horses were driven home immediately thereafter.
   D. The attorney asked my wife and myself several questions.

6.____

7. A. Despite all denials, there is no doubt in my mind that
   B. At this time everyone must deprecate the demogogic attack made by one of our Senators on one of our most revered statesmen.
   C. In the first game of a crucial two-game series, Ted Williams, got two singles, both of them driving in a run.
   D. Our visitor brought good news to John and I.

7.____

8. A. If he would have told me, I should have been glad to help him in his dire financial emergency.
   B. Newspaper men have often asserted that diplomats or so-called official spokesmen sometimes employ equivocation in attempts to deceive.
   C. I think someones coming to collect money for the Red Cross.
   D. In a masterly summation, the young attorney expressed his belief that the facts clearly militate against this opinion.

8.____

9. A. We have seen most all the exhibits.
   B. Without in the least underestimating your advice, in my opinion the situation has grown immeasurably worse in the past few days.
   C. I wrote to the box office treasurer of the hit show that a pair of orchestra seats would be preferable.
   D. As the grim story of Pearl Harbor was broadcast on that fateful December 7, it was the general opinion that war was inevitable.

9.____

10. A. Without a moment's hesitation, Casey Stengel said that Larry Berra works harder than any player on the team.
    B. There is ample evidence to indicate that many animals can run faster than any human being.
    C. No one saw the accident but I.
    D. Example of courage is the heroic defense put up by the paratroopers against overwhelming odds.

10.____

11. A. If you prefer these kind, Mrs. Grey, we shall be more than willing to let you have them reasonably.
    B. If you like these here, Mrs. Grey, we shall be more than willing to let you have them reasonably.
    C. If you like these, Mrs. Grey, we shall be more than willing to let you have them.
    D. Who shall we appoint?

11.____

3 (#2)

12. A. The number of errors are greater in speech than in writing. 12.____
    B. The doctor rather than the nurse was to blame for his being neglected.
    C. Because the demand for these books have been so great, we reduced the price.
    D. John Galsworthy, the English novelist, could not have survived a serious illness; had it not been for loving care.

13. A. Our activities this year have seldom ever been as interesting as they have been this month. 13.____
    B. Our activities this month have been more interesting, or at least as interesting as those of any month this year.
    C. Our activities this month has been more interesting than those of any other month this year.
    D. Neither Jean nor her sister was at home.

14. A. George B. Shaw's view of common morality, as well as his wit sparkling with a dash of perverse humor here and there, have led critics to term him "The Incurable Rebel." 14.____
    B. The President's program was not always received with the wholehearted endorsement of his own party, which is why the party faces difficulty in drawing up a platform for the coming election.
    C. The reason why they wanted to travel was because they had never been away from home.
    D. Facing a barrage of cameras, the visiting celebrity found it extremely difficult to express his opinions clearly.

15. A. When we calmed down, we all agreed that our anger had been kind of unnecessary and had not helped the situation. 15.____
    B. Without him going into all the details, he made us realize the horror of the accident.
    C. Like one girl, for example, who applied for two positions.
    D. Do not think that you have to be so talented as he is in order to play in the school orchestra.

16. A. He looked very peculiarly to me. 16.____
    B. He certainly looked at me peculiar.
    C. Due to the train's being late, we had to wait an hour.
    D. The reason for the poor attendance is that it is raining.

17. A. About one out of four own an automobile. 17.____
    B. The collapse of the old Mitchell Bridge was caused by defective construction in the central pier.
    C. Brooks Atkinson was well acquainted with the best literature, thus helping him to become an able critic.
    D. He has to stand still until the relief man comes up, thus giving him no chance to move about and keep warm.

18. A. He is sensitive to confusion and withdraws from people whom he feels are too noisy.
    B. Do you know whether the data is statistically correct?
    C. Neither the mayor or the aldermen are to blame.
    D. Of those who were graduated from high school, a goodly percentage went to college.

18.____

19. A. Acting on orders, the offices were searched by a designated committee.
    B. The answer probably is nothing.
    C. I thought it to be all right to excuse them from class.
    D. I think that he is as successful a singer, if not more successful, than Mary.

19.____

20. A. $360,000 is really very little to pay for such a wellbuilt house.
    B. The creatures looked like they had come from outer space.
    C. It was her, he knew!
    D. Nobody but me knows what to do.

20.____

21. A. Mrs. Smith looked good in her new suit.
    B. New York may be compared with Chicago.
    C. I will not go to the meeting except you go with me.
    D. I agree with this editorial.

21.____

22. A. My opinions are different from his.
    B. There will be less students in class now.
    C. Helen was real glad to find her watch.
    D. It had been pushed off of her dresser.

22.____

23. A. Almost everyone, who has been to California, returns with glowing reports.
    B. George Washington, John Adams, and Thomas Jefferson, were our first presidents.
    C. Mr. Walters, whom we met at the bank yesterday, is the man, who gave me my first job.
    D. One should study his lessons as carefully as he can.

23.____

24. A. We had such a good time yesterday.
    B. When the bell rang, the boys and girls went in the schoolhouse.
    C. John had the worst headache when he got up this morning.
    D. Today's assignment is somewhat longer than yesterday's.

24.____

25. A. Neither the mayor nor the city clerk are willing to talk.
    B. Neither the mayor nor the city clerk is willing to talk.
    C. Neither the mayor or the city clerk are willing to talk.
    D Neither the mayor or the city clerk is willing to talk.

25.____

26. A. Being that he is that kind of boy, cooperation cannot be expected.
    B. He interviewed people who he thought had something to say.
    C. Stop whomever enters the building regardless of rank or office held.
    D. Passing through the countryside, the scenery pleased us.

26.____

27. A. The childrens' shoes were in their closet. 27.____
    B. The children's shoes were in their closet.
    C. The childs' shoes were in their closet.
    D. The childs' shoes were in his closet.

28. A. An agreement was reached between the defendant, the plaintiff, the 28.____
       plaintiff's attorney and the insurance company as to the amount of the
       settlement.
    B. Everybody was asked to give their versions of the accident.
    C. The consensus of opinion was that the evidence was inconclusive.
    D. The witness stated that if he was rich, he wouldn't have had to loan the
       money.

29. A. Before beginning the investigation, all the materials related to the case were 29.____
       carefully assembled.
    B. The reason for his inability to keep the appointment is because of his injury
       in the accident.
    C. This here evidence tends to support the claim of the defendant.
    D. We interviewed all the witnesses who, according to the driver, were still in
       town.

30. A. Each claimant was allowed the full amount of their medical expenses. 30.____
    B. Either of the three witnesses is available.
    C. Every one of the witnesses was asked to tell his story.
    D. Neither of the witnesses are right.

31. A. The commissioner, as well as his deputy and various bureau heads, were 31.____
       present.
    B. A new organization of employers and employees have been formed.
    C. One or the other of these men have been selected.
    D. The number of pages in the book is enough to discourage a reader.

32. A. Between you and me, I think he is the better man. 32.____
    B. He was believed to be me.
    C. Is it us that you wish to see?
    D. The winners are him and her.

33. A. Beside the statement to the police, the witness spoke to no one. 33.____
    B. He made no statement other than to the police and I.
    C. He made no statement to any one else, aside from the police.
    D. The witness spoke to no one but me.

34. A. The claimant has no one to blame but himself. 34.____
    B. The boss sent us, he and I, to deliver the packages.
    C. The lights come from mine and not his car.
    D. There was room on the stairs for him and myself.

35. A. Admission to this clinic is limited to patients' inability to pay for medical care.
    B. Patients who can pay little or nothing for medical care are treated in this clinic.
    C. The patient's ability to pay for medical care is the determining factor in his admission to this clinic.
    D. This clinic is for the patient's that cannot afford to pay or that can pay a little for medical care.

35.____

KEY (CORRECT ANSWERS)

1.	A	11.	C	21.	A	31.	D
2.	A	12.	B	22.	A	32.	A
3.	D	13.	D	23.	D	33.	D
4.	C	14.	D	24.	D	34.	A
5.	D	15.	D	25.	B	35.	B
6.	D	16.	D	26.	B		
7.	B	17.	B	27.	B		
8.	B	18.	D	28.	C		
9.	D	19.	B	29.	D		
10.	B	20.	D	30.	C		

EXAMINATION SECTION
TEST 1

DIRECTIONS: Each of the following sentences, as written, is grammatically incorrect for one or more reasons. Rewrite the sentences in CORRECT grammatical form, making as few changes as possible from the original text.

1. I did not know how to reply when he wanted to know was I going to assist him in the undertaking.

2. You will observe not only the rules in the book, but you will use your common sense as well.

3. The change in his condition is distinctly for the better due to the hard work of the doctor and the nurse.

4. If he will come before I leave, I will give him your message.

5. Hitch your wagon to a star and ride, ride till the sun.

6. The judge declared that neither the policeman nor the man whom he had arrested were telling the whole truth.

7. The reason why the sunspots cause changes in the weather is because they are electric disturbances.

8. Bring this book to the library in order that you will not have to pay an accumulated fine.

9. He had laid so long in bed that he found it difficult to move about normally.

10. He wanted us to slowly and carefully pour the oil into the smaller bottles.

KEY (CORRECT ANSWERS)

1. I did not know how to reply when he wanted to know whether I was going to assist him in the undertaking.

2. Not only will you observe the rules in the book, but you will use your common sense as well.

3. The change in his condition is distinctly for the better because of the hard work of the doctor and the nurse.

4. If he comes before I leave, I will give him your message.

5. Hitch your wagon to a star and ride, ride to the sun.

6. The judge declared that neither the policeman nor the man whom he had arrested was telling the whole truth.

7. The reason why the sunspots cause changes in the weather is that they are electric disturbances.

8. Take this book to the library in order that you will not have to pay an accumulated fine.

9. He had lain so long in bed that he found it difficult to move about normally.

10. He wanted us to pour the oil slowly and carefully into the smaller bottles.

TEST 2

DIRECTIONS: Each of the following sentences, as written, is grammatically incorrect for one or more reasons. Rewrite the sentences in CORRECT grammatical form, making as few changes as possible from the original text.

1. We could not be sure if he meant to be present or was just politely suggesting that he might come.

2. They tell me that the coaches invite only such members of the freshman class who are apt to prove good material in their upper years.

3. We found less persons on the beach after the storm than at any other time.

4. We asked permission to partake in the activities, but we were refused.

5. Appreciating our good luck, the play for which we had received free tickets, seemed doubly interesting.

6. The book he recommended was different than the one you bought for me.

7. Thousands and thousands of young men and women graduate our colleges annually.

8. One can never say that the person whom you know is a friend of yours one day, will be your friend the next.

9. Their's not to reason why is a famous quote from a poem by Tennyson.

10. If not for his father's timely advice, he would have left school.

KEY (CORRECT ANSWERS)

1. We could not be sure whether he meant to be present or was just politely suggesting that he might come.

2. They tell me that the coaches invite only such members of the freshman class as are apt to prove good material in their upper years.

3. We found fewer persons on the beach after the storm than at any other time.

4. We asked permission to take part in the activities, but we were refused.

5. Since we appreciated our good luck, the play for which we had received free tickets seemed doubly interesting.

6. The book he recommended was different from the one you bought for me.

7. Thousands and thousands of young men and women are graduated from our colleges annually.

8. One can never say that the person who you know is your friend today, will be your friend tomorrow.

9. Theirs not to reason why is a famous quotation from a poem by Tennyson.

10. Had it not been for his father's timely advice, he would have left school.

TEST 3

DIRECTIONS: Each of the following sentences, as written, is grammatically incorrect for one or more reasons. Rewrite the sentences in CORRECT grammatical form, making as few changes as possible from the original text.

1. He went to the concert so often before, that he did not care to go that night.

2. Although he claimed that all his jewels and cash had been robbed, he did not seem to be the least bit worried.

3. Well what are you going to do now without your equipment and gear.

4. Let us all get the true facts first; then we can reach a decision.

5. We bought a book suitable for you, but which I would not think of reading.

6. While waiting for my friend to appear, a telephone message from him arrived.

7. He certainly deserves to be punished: still and all I feel sorry for him.

8. Cheating on an examination is as foolish as to conceal your symptoms from the doctor.

9. I consider aviation a very hazardous occupation, but being that you have set your heart on learning how to fly, I shall say no more in regard(s) to your decision.

10. Her appearance was not only striking, but she had an interesting personality as well.

KEY (CORRECT ANSWERS)

1. He had gone to the concert so often before that he did not care to go that night.

2. Although he claimed that all his jewels and cash had been stolen, he did not seem to be the least bit worried.

3. Well, what are you going to do now without your equipment and gear?

4. Let us all get the facts first; then we can reach a decision.

5. We bought a book suitable for you but one which I would not think of reading.

6. While I was waiting for my friend to appear, a telephone message from him arrived.

7. He certainly deserves to be punished; nevertheless, I feel sorry for him.

8. Cheating on an examination is as foolish as concealing your symptoms from the doctor.

9. I consider aviation a very hazardous occupation, but since you have set your heart on learning how to fly, I shall say no more in regard to your decision.

10. Not only was her appearance striking, but she had an interesting personality as well.

TEST 4

DIRECTIONS: Each of the following sentences, as written, is grammatically incorrect for one or more reasons. Rewrite the sentences in CORRECT grammatical form, making as few changes as possible from the original text.

1. Walking up Broadway from Fulton Street, the Woolworth Building strikes the observer.

2. Imagine a person risking his life to so dramatically save the day.

3. We expect to go irregardless of the weather clearing up.

4. The jar was so full that he had to spill some of the water in the sink.

5. George Washington the man who everyone admires was keenly alive to every opportunity.

6. Queen Elizabeth as the story goes was once very much in love with Essex.

7. The Nebular Hypothesis LaPlace's famous theory is not universally accepted.

8. The crew had no sooner removed the last passenger when the ship sunk.

9. Whom do you expect him to be was the question put to the defendant.

10. You said you should probably go by train.

2 (#4)

KEY (CORRECT ANSWERS)

1. As he walks up Broadway from Fulton Street, the Woolworth Building strikes the observer.

2. Imagine a person's risking his life to save the day so dramatically.

3. We expect to go regardless of the weather clearing up.

4. The jar was so full that we had to pour some of the water into the sink.

5. George Washington, the man whom everyone admires, was keenly alive to every opportunity.

6. Queen Elizabeth, as the story goes, was once very much in love with Essex.

7. The Nebular Hypothesis, La Place's famous theory, is not universally accepted.

8. The crew had no sooner removed the last passenger than the ship sank.

9. "Whom do you expect him to be?" was the question put to the defendant.

10. You said you would probably go by train.

TEST 5

DIRECTIONS: Each of the following sentences, as written, is grammatically incorrect for one or more reasons. Rewrite the sentence in CORRECT grammatical form, making as few changes as possible from the original text.

1. The rotation plan is used in office practice classes, largely due to the fact that there is insufficient equipment.

2. This calls for the purchase of a large number of machines which is practically impossible from an economy standpoint.

3. The advantages of such an arrangement enables the teacher to plan her work more efficiently.

4. There is a stigma attached to being in a slow group and danger of pupils in a bright group from becoming conceited.

5. There are administrative details that can only be worked out with the sympathetic cooperation of the principal.

6. For instance if there were only an average and a bright class, the slow pupils would be put into the average.

7. Pupils and parents would object to a child being classified "slow". This has not been difficult to overcome where the plan has been tried.

8. The second and third Epistle of John contain each a single chapter.

9. It boils down to this: either you or I are right.

10. No time, no money, no labor was spared to make the fair an artistic success.

2 (#5)

KEY (CORRECT ANSWERS)

1. The rotation plan is used in office practice classes largely because of the fact that there is insufficient equipment.

2. This calls for the purchase of a large number of machines. Such a purchase is practically impossible from an economy standpoint.

3. The advantages of such an arrangement is that it enables the teacher to plan her work more efficiently.

4. There is a stigma attached to being in a slow group and a danger that the pupils in a bright group might become conceited.

5. There are administrative details that can be worked out only with the sympathetic cooperation of the principal.

6. For instance, if there were only an average and a bright class, the slow pupils would be put into the average class.

7. Pupils and parents would object to a child's being classified "slow." This has not been difficult to overcome when the plan has been tried.

8. Each of the second and third Epistles of John consists of a single chapter.

9. It boils down to this: either you or I am right.

10. No time, no money, no labor were spared to make the fair an artistic one.

TEST 6

DIRECTIONS: Each of the following sentences, as written, is grammatically incorrect for one or more reasons. Rewrite the sentence in CORRECT grammatical form, making as few changes as possible from the original text.

1. Bread is more nutritious, but not so cheap, as potatoes.

2. This dedication may serve for almost any book that has, is, or may be published.

3. Mr. Asquith concluded on a note of high appeal for the substitution of the Supreme Council by the League of Nations.

4. The municipality purchased these articles in wholesale quantities and it was to the Town Hall that people applied for them and were served by municipal employees.

5. There is a distinction between the man who gives with conviction and he who is simply buying a title.

6. Because his manners were exceptionable he was invited most every where by the elite of the town.

7. If I'd have gone about collecting this data as quick as you desired, the job would now be finished.

8. Inside of a week the thieves broke in his house twice.

9. Don't be angry at me for losing your book; this one is as new or newer than yours.

10. It was none other but Morgan; the reason he left so suddenly was because he feared the discovery of the plot.

KEY (CORRECT ANSWERS)

1. Bread is more nutritious than potatoes but not so cheap.

2. This dedication may serve for almost any book that has been or may be published.

3. Mr. Asquith concluded on a high note of appeal for the substitution of the Supreme Council by the League of Nations.

4. The municipality purchased these articles in wholesale quantities, and it was at the Town Hall that people applied for them and were served by municipal employees.

5. There is a distinction between the man who gives with conviction and him who is simply buying a title.

6. Because his manners were unexceptionable he was invited almost everywhere by the elite of the town.

7. If I had gone about collecting these data as quickly as you desired, the job would now be finished.

8. Within a week the thieves broke into his house twice.

9. Don't be angry at me for losing your book; this one is as new as or newer than yours.

10. It was none other than Morgan; the reason he left so suddenly was that he feared the discovery of the plot.

TEST 7

DIRECTIONS: Each of the following sentences, as written, is grammatically incorrect for one or more reasons. Rewrite the sentence in CORRECT grammatical form, making as few changes as possible from the original text.

1. Due to his poor management, I found conditions different to what I expected, even though he was enamored by his work.

2. One need not take examinations preliminary for college entrance, providing your scholastic record is high enough to exempt you from them.

3. I do not like this passage, but leave it stay in the examination.

4. A duel is when two persons fight to settle a quarrel that has risen according to certain rules.

5. "Will you be glad to see us?" He had ought to know what my answer would be.

6. A big gray cat dashed across the road.

7. We saw many wonderful things for example, a carved sun dial.

8. By August he shall be living in New York for ten years.

9. Madame Curie was the cleverest of most women of her time.

10. If the book is laying on my desk, will you send it to the library for me, please?

KEY (CORRECT ANSWERS)

1. Because of his poor management, I found conditions different from what I had expected, even though he was enamored of his work.

2. One need not take preliminary examinations for college entrance, provided that your scholastic record is high enough to exempt you from them.

3. I do not like this passage, but let it stay in the examination.

4. A duel occurs when two persons fight according to certain rules to settle a quarrel that has arisen.

5. "Shall you be glad to see us?" He ought to have known what my answer would be.

6. A big, gray cat dashed across the road.

7. We saw many wonderful things; for example, a carved sun dial.

8. By August he will have lived in New York ten years.

9. Madame Curie was cleverer than most women of her time.

10. If the book is lying on my desk, will you send it to the library for me, please?

TEST 8

DIRECTIONS: Each of the following sentences, as written, is grammatically incorrect for one or more reasons. Rewrite the sentences in CORRECT grammatical form, making as few changes as possible from the original text.

1. It is an insult to I who am your friend.//
2. Every one of the spectators were ready to declare they thought it cruel.
3. We passed over the road quickly and soon the camp was reached.
4. He is almost the handsomest man I ever saw.
5. The person who steals in nine cases out of ten is driven by hunger.
6. He is one of the greatest, if not the greatest lawyers of America.
7. John as well as his brother is going to the party.
8. The storm was already at hand, I had no time to eat.
9. Dr. Brown, who was to be here yesterday, left a prescription for me.
10. He bought nails, bolts, locks, and etc.

KEY (CORRECT ANSWERS)

1. It is an insult to me who am your friend.//
2. Every one of the spectators was ready to declare he thought it cruel.
3. We passed over the road quickly and soon reached the camp.
4. He is perhaps the handsomest man I have ever seen.
5. The person who steals is, in nine cases out of ten, driven by hunger.
6. He is one of the greatest lawyers of America, if not the greatest.
7. John, as well as his brother, is going to the party.
8. The storm was already at hand: I had no time to eat.
9. Dr. Brown, who was here yesterday, left a prescription for me.
10. He bought nails, bolts, locks, etc.

TEST 9

DIRECTIONS: Each of the following sentences, as written, is grammatically incorrect for one or more reasons. Rewrite the sentences in CORRECT grammatical form, making as few changes as possible from the original text.

1. I like books on the whole, but these kind of books always bores me.

2. Is there any chance of you leaving the city this summer?

3. Many important events had happened since I wrote that news article.

4. I lie awake all night thinking of the future.

5. He admitted those only with tickets.

6. Favored by a warm winter climate, I regard Florida as a popular resort.

7. After hearing modern jazz, all other music sounds dull.

8. He has two friends to help him now, John and she.

9. This pen may be carried by anyone, everywhere, without danger of it leaking.

10. It was easiest to purchase gifts for her than me.

2 (#9)

KEY (CORRECT ANSWERS)

1. I like books on the whole, but this kind of book always bores me.

2. Is there any chance of your leaving the city this summer?

3. Many important events have happened since I wrote that news article.

4. I lay awake all night thinking of the future.

5. He admitted only those with tickets.

6. Favored by a warm winter climate, Florida is a popular resort.

7. After hearing modern jazz, I feel that all other music sounds dull.

8. He has two friends to help him now, John and her.

9. This pen may be carried by anyone, everywhere, without danger of its leaking.

10. It was easier to purchase gifts for her than me.

TEST 10

DIRECTIONS: Each of the following sentences, as written, is grammatically incorrect for one or more reasons. Rewrite the sentences in CORRECT grammatical form, making as few changes as possible from the original text.

1. The book is about a peddler whom all the Americans thought was an English spy.

2. Bad news travel fast.

3. We must strive to attain academic freedom irregardless of personal consequences.

4. He promised that he might deliver the car on September first, but he did not say which year.

5. You must proceed slow with difficult experiments.

6. They advise others to take the same course that they have.

7. Without noticing, they ride past their station.

8. If I was you, I should wait for them.

9. That he is wrong, he already knows.

10. The richness of his apparel and arms were conspicuous.

KEY (CORRECT ANSWERS)

1. The book is about a peddler who all the Americans thought was an English spy.
2. Bad news travels fast.
3. We must strive to attain academic freedom regardless of personal consequences.
4. He promised that he would deliver the car on September first, but he did not say which year.
5. You must proceed slowly with difficult experiments.
6. They advised others to take the same course that they had taken.
7. Without noticing, they rode past their station.
8. If I were you, I should wait for them.
9. That he was wrong, he already knows.
10. The richness of his apparel and arms was conspicuous.

PREPARING WRITTEN MATERIAL
EXAMINATION SECTION
TEST 1

DIRECTIONS: Each question consists of a sentence which may or may not be an example of good English usage. Examine each sentence, considering grammar, punctuation, spelling, capitalization, and awkwardness. Then choose the correct statement about it from the four choices below it. If the English usage in the sentence given is better than any of the changes suggested in choices B, C, or D, pick choice A. (Do not pick a choice that will change the meaning of the sentence.) *PRINT THE LETTER OF THE CORRECT ANSWER IN THE SPACE AT THE RIGHT.*

1. We attended a staff conference on Wednesday the new safety and fire rules were discussed. 1.____
    A. This is an example of acceptable writing.
    B. The words "safety," "fire," and "rules" should begin with capital letters.
    C. There should be a comma after the word "Wednesday."
    D. There should be a period after the word "Wednesday" and the word "the" should begin with a capital letter.

2. Neither the dictionary or the telephone directory could be found in the office library. 2.____
    A. This is an example of acceptable writing.
    B. The word "or" should be changed to "nor."
    C. The word "library" should be spelled "libery."
    D. The word "neither" should be changed to "either."

3. The report would have been typed correctly if the typist could read the draft. 3.____
    A. This is an example of acceptable writing.
    B. The word "would" should be removed.
    C. The word "have" should be inserted after the word "could."
    D. The word "correctly" should be changed to "correct."

4. The supervisor brought the reports and forms to an employees desk. 4.____
    A. This is an example of acceptable writing.
    B. The word "brought" should be changed to "took."
    C. There should be a comma after the word "reports" and a comma after the word "forms."
    D. The word "employees" should be spelled "employee's."

5. It's important for all the office personnel to submit their vacation schedules on time. 5.____
    A. This is an example of acceptable writing.
    B. The word "It's" should be spelled "Its."
    C. The word "their" should be spelled "they're."
    D. The word "personnel" should be spelled "personal."

6. The report, along with the accompanying documents, were submitted for review.
    A. This is an example of acceptable writing.
    B. The words "were submitted" should be changed to "was submitted."
    C. The word "accompanying" should be spelled "accompaning."
    D. The comma after the word "report" should be taken out.

    6.____

7. If others must use your files, be certain that they understand how the system works, but insist that you do all the filing and refiling.
    A. This is an example of acceptable writing.
    B. There should be a period after the word "works," and the word "but" should start a new sentence.
    C. The words "filing" and "refiling" should be spelled "fileing" and "refileing."
    D. There should be a comma after the word "but."

    7.____

8. The appeal was not considered because of its late arrival.
    A. This is an example of acceptable writing.
    B. The word "its" should be changed to "it's."
    C. The word "its" should be changed to "the."
    D. The words "late arrival" should be changed to "arrival late."

    8.____

9. The letter must be read carefuly to determine under which subject it should be filed.
    A. This is an example of acceptable writing.
    B. The word "under" should be changed to "at."
    C. The word "determine" should be spelled "determin."
    D. The word "carefuly" should be spelled "carefully."

    9.____

10. He showed potential as an office manager, but he lacked skill in delegating work.
    A. This is an example of acceptable writing.
    B. The word "delegating" should be spelled "delagating."
    C. The word "potential" should be spelled "potencial."
    D. The words "he lacked" should be changed to "was lacking."

    10.____

KEY (CORRECT ANSWERS)

1.	D	6.	B
2.	B	7.	A
3.	C	8.	A
4.	D	9.	D
5.	A	10.	A

TEST 2

DIRECTIONS: Each question consists of a sentence which may or may not be an example of good English usage. Examine each sentence, considering grammar, punctuation, spelling, capitalization, and awkwardness. Then choose the correct statement about it from the four choices below it. If the English usage in the sentence given is better than any of the changes suggested in choices B, C, or D, pick choice A. (Do not pick a choice that will change the meaning of the sentence.) *PRINT THE LETTER OF THE CORRECT ANSWER IN THE SPACE AT THE RIGHT.*

1. The supervisor wants that all staff members report to the office at 9:00 A.M.   1.____
    A. This is an example of acceptable writing.
    B. The word "that" should be removed and the word "to" should be inserted after the word "members."
    C. There should be a comma after the word "wants" and a comma after the word "office."
    D. The word "wants" should be changed to "want" and the word "shall" should be inserted after the word "members."

2. Every morning the clerk opens the office mail and distributes it.   2.____
    A. This is an example of acceptable writing.
    B. The word "opens" should be changed to "open."
    C. The word "mail" should be changed to "letters."
    D. The word "it" should be changed to "them."

3. The secretary typed more fast on a desktop computer than on a laptop computer.   3.____
    A. This is an example of acceptable writing.
    B. The words "more fast" should be changed to "faster."
    C. There should be a comma after the words "desktop computer."
    D. The word "than" should be changed to "then."

4. The new stenographer needed a desk a computer, a chair and a blotter.   4.____
    A. This is an example of acceptable writing.
    B. The word "blotter" should be spelled "blodder."
    C. The word "stenographer" should begin with a capital letter.
    D. There should be a comma after the word "desk."

5. The recruiting officer said, "There are many different goverment jobs available."   5.____
    A. This is an example of acceptable writing.
    B. The word "There" should not be capitalized.
    C. The word "government" should be spelled "government."
    D. The comma after the word "said" should be removed.

6. He can recommend a mechanic whose work is reliable.   6.____
    A. This is an example of acceptable writing.
    B. The word "reliable" should be spelled "relyable."
    C. The word "whose" should be spelled "who's."
    D. The word "mechanic should be spelled "mecanic."

7. She typed quickly; like someone who had not a moment to lose. 7._____
   A. This is an example of acceptable writing.
   B. The word "not" should be removed.
   C. The semicolon should be changed to a comma.
   D. The word "quickly" should be placed before instead of after the word "typed."

8. She insisted that she had to much work to do. 8._____
   A. This is an example of acceptable writing.
   B. The word "insisted" should be spelled "incisted."
   C. The word "to" used in front of "much" should be spelled "too."
   D. The word "do" should be changed to "be done."

9. He excepted praise from his supervisor for a job well done. 9._____
   A. This is an example of acceptable writing.
   B. The word "excepted" should be spelled "accepted."
   C. The order of the words "well done" should be changed to "done well."
   D. There should be a comma after the word "supervisor."

10. What appears to be intentional errors in grammar occur several times in the passage. 10._____
    A. This is an example of acceptable writing.
    B. The word "occur" should be spelled "occurr."
    C. The word "appears" should be changed to "appear."
    D. The phrase "several times" should be changed to "from time to time."

KEY (CORRECT ANSWERS)

1.	B	6.	A
2.	A	7.	C
3.	B	8.	C
4.	D	9.	B
5.	C	10.	C

TEST 3

DIRECTIONS: Each question consists of a sentence which may or may not be an example of good English usage. Examine each sentence, considering grammar, punctuation, spelling, capitalization, and awkwardness. Then choose the correct statement about it from the four choices below it. If the English usage in the sentence given is better than any of the changes suggested in choices B, C, or D, pick choice A. (Do not pick a choice that will change the meaning of the sentence.) *PRINT THE LETTER OF THE CORRECT ANSWER IN THE SPACE AT THE RIGHT.*

1. The clerk could have completed the assignment on time if he knows where these materials were located.
   A. This is an example of acceptable writing.
   B. The word "knows" should be replaced by "had known."
   C. The word "were" should be replaced by "had been."
   D. The words "where these materials were located" should be replaced by "the location of these materials."

   1.____

2. All employees should be given safety training. Not just those who accidents.
   A. This is an example of acceptable writing.
   B. The period after the word "training" should be changed to a colon.
   C. The period after the word "training" should be changed to a semicolon, and the first letter of the word "Not" should be changed to a small "n."
   D. The period after the word "training" should be changed to a comma, and the first letter of the word "Not" should be changed to a small "n."

   2.____

3. This proposal is designed to promote employee awareness of the suggestion program, to encourage employee participation in the program, and to increase the number of suggestions submitted.
   A. This is an example of acceptable writing.
   B. The word "proposal" should be spelled "proposal."
   C. The words "to increase the number of suggestions submitted" should be changed to "an increase in the number of suggestions is expected."
   D. The word "promote" should be changed to "enhance" and the word "increase" should be changed to "add to."

   3.____

4. The introduction of inovative managerial techniques should be preceded by careful analysis of the specific circumstances and conditions in each department.
   A. This is an example of acceptable writing.
   B. The word "technique" should be spelled "techneques."
   C. The word "inovative" should be spelled "innovative."
   D. A comma should be placed after the word "circumstances" and after the word "conditions."

   4.____

139

5. This occurrence indicates that such criticism embarrasses him. 5.____
    A. This is an example of acceptable writing.
    B. The word "occurrence" should be spelled "occurence."
    C. The word "criticism" should be spelled "critisism.
    D. The word "embarrasses" should be spelled "embarasses.

KEY (CORRECT ANSWERS)

1. B
2. D
3. A
4. C
5. A

PREPARING WRITTEN MATERIAL

PARAGRAPH REARRANGEMENT
COMMENTARY

The sentences that follow are in scrambled order. You are to rearrange them in proper order and indicate the letter choice containing the correct answer at the space at the right.

Each group of sentences in this section is actually a paragraph presented in scrambled order. Each sentence in the group has a place in that paragraph; no sentence is to be left out. You are to read each group of sentences and decide upon the best order in which to put the sentences so as to form a well-organized paragraph.

The questions in this section measure the ability to solve a problem when all the facts relevant to its solution are not given.

More specifically, certain positions of responsibility and authority require the employee to discover connection between events sometimes, apparently, unrelated. In order to do this, the employee will find it necessary to correctly infer that unspecified events have probably occurred or are likely to occur. This ability becomes especially important when action must be taken on incomplete information.

Accordingly, these questions require competitors to choose among several suggested alternatives, each of which presents a different sequential arrangement of the events. Competitors must choose the MOST logical of the suggested sequences.

In order to do so, they may be required to draw on general knowledge to infer missing concepts or events that are essential to sequencing the given events. Competitors should be careful to infer only what is essential to the sequence. The plausibility of the wrong alternatives will always require the inclusion of unlikely events or of additional chains of events which are NOT essential to sequencing the given events.

It's very important to remember that you are looking for the best of the four possible choices, and that the best choice of all may not even be one of the answers you're given to choose from.

There is no one right way to solve these problems. Many people have found it helpful to first write out the order of the sentences, as they would have arranged them, on their scrap paper before looking at the possible answers. If their optimum answer is there, this can save them some time. If it isn't, this method can still give insight into solving the problem. Others find it most helpful to just go through each of the possible choices, contrasting each as they go along. You should use whatever method feels comfortable and works for you.

While most of these types of questions are not that difficult, we've added a higher percentage of the difficult type, just to give you more practice. Usually there are only one or two questions on this section that contain such subtle distinctions that you're unable to answer confidently. And you then may find yourself stuck deciding between two possible choices, neither of which you're sure about.

EXAMINATION SECTION

TEST 1

DIRECTIONS: The following groups of sentences need to be arranged in an order that makes sense. Select the letter preceding the sequence that represents the BEST sentence order. *PRINT THE LETTER OF THE CORRECT ANSWER IN THE SPACE AT THE RIGHT.*

1. I. The keyboard was purposely designed to be a little awkward to slow typists down.
   II. The arrangement of letters on the keyboard of a typewriter was not designed for the convenience of the typist.
   III. Fortunately, no one is suggesting that a new keyboard be designed right away.
   IV. If one were, we would have to learn to type all over again.
   V. The reason was that the early machines were slower than the typists and would jam easily.
   The CORRECT answer is:
   A. I, III, IV, II, V
   B. II, V, I, IV, III
   C. V, I, II, III, IV
   D. II, I, V, III, IV

   1.____

2. I. The majority of the new service jobs are part-time or low-paying.
   II. According to the U.S. Bureau of Labor Statistics, jobs in the service sector constitute 72% of all jobs in this country.
   III. If more and more workers receive less and less money, who will buy the goods and services needed to keep the economy going?
   IV. The service sector is by far the fastest growing part of the United States economy.
   V. Some economists look upon this trend with great concern.
   The CORRECT answer is:
   A. II, IV, I, V, III
   B. II, III, IV, I, V
   C. V, IV, II, III, I
   D. III, I, II, IV, V

   2.____

3. I. They can also affect one's endurance.
   II. This can stabilize blood sugar levels, and ensure that the brain is receiving a steady, constant, supply of glucose, so that one is *hitting on all cylinders* while taking the test.
   III. By food, we mean real food, not junk food or unhealthy snacks.
   IV. For this reason, it is important not to skip a meal, and to bring food with you to the exam.
   V. One's blood sugar levels can affect how clearly one is able to think and concentrate during an exam.
   The CORRECT answer is:
   A. V, IV, II, III, I
   B. V, II, I, IV, III
   C. V, I, IV, III, II
   D. V, IV, I, III, II

   3.____

143

4. I. Those who are the embodiment of desire are absorbed in material quests, and those who are the embodiment of feeling are warriors who value power more than possession.
   II. These qualities are in everyone, but in different degrees.
   III. But those who value understanding yearn not for goods or victory, but for knowledge.
   IV. According to Plato, human behavior flows from three main sources: desire, emotion, and knowledge.
   V. In the perfect state, the industrial forces would produce but not rule, the military would protect but not rule, and the forces of knowledge, the philosopher kings, would reign.
   The CORRECT answer is:
   A. IV, V, I, II, III
   B. V, I, II, III, IV
   C. IV, III, II, I, V
   D. IV, II, I, III, V

   4.____

5. I. Of the more than 26,000 tons of garbage produced daily in New York City, 12,000 tons arrive daily at Fresh Kills.
   II. In a month, enough garbage accumulates there to fill the Empire State Building.
   III. In 1937, the Supreme Court halted the practice of dumping the trash of New York City into the sea.
   IV. Although the garbage is compacted, in a few years the mounds of garbage at Fresh Kills will be the highest points south of Maine's Mount Desert Island on the Eastern Seaboard.
   V. Instead, tugboats now pull barges of much of the trash to Staten Island and the largest landfill in the world, Fresh Kills.
   The CORRECT answer is:
   A. III, V, IV, I, II
   B. III, V, II, IV, I
   C. III, V, I, II, IV
   D. III, II, V, IV, I

   5.____

6. I. Communists rank equality very high, but freedom very low.
   II. Unlike communists, conservatives place a high value on freedom and a very low value on equality.
   III. A recent study demonstrated that one way to classify people's political beliefs is to look at the importance placed on two words: freedom and equality.
   IV. Thus, by demonstrating how members of these groups feel about the two words, the study has proved to be useful for political analysts in several European countries.
   V. According to the study, socialists and liberals rank both freedom and equality very high, while fascists rate both very low.
   The CORRECT answer is:
   A. III, V, I, II, IV
   B. V, IV, III, I, II
   C. III, V, IV, II, I
   D. III, I, II, IV, V

   6.____

7. I. "Can there be anything more amazing than this?"
    II. If the riddle is successfully answered, his dead brothers will be brought back to life.
    III. "Even though man sees those around him dying every day," says Dharmaraj, "he still believes and acts as if he were immortal."
    IV. "What is the cause of ceaseless wonder?" asks the Lord of the Lake.
    V. In the ancient epic, The Mahabharata, a riddle is asked of one of the Pandava brothers.
    The CORRECT answer is:
    A. V, II, I, IV, III
    B. V, IV, III, I, II
    C. V, II, IV, III, I
    D. V, II, IV, I, III

    7.____

8. I. On the contrary, the two main theories—the cooperative (neoclassical) theory and the radical (labor theory)—clearly rest on very different assumptions, which have very different ethical overtones.
    II. The distribution of income is the primary factor in determining the relative levels of material well-being that different groups or individuals attain.
    III. Of all issues in economics, the distribution of income is one of the most controversial.
    IV. The neoclassical theory tends to support the existing income distribution (or minor changes), while the labor theory ends to support substantial changes in the way income is distributed.
    V. The intensity of the controversy reflects the fact that different economic theories are not purely neutral, *detached* theories with no ethical or moral implications.
    The CORRECT answer is:
    A. II, I, V, IV, III
    B. III, II, V, I, IV
    C. III, V, II, I, IV
    D. III, V, IV, I, II

    8.____

9. I. The pool acts as a broker and ensures that the cheapest power gets used first.
    II. Every six seconds, the pool's computer monitors all of the generating stations in the state and decides which to ask for more power and which to cut back.
    III. The buying and selling of electrical power is handled by the New York Power Pool in Guilderland, New York.
    IV. This is to the advantage of both the buying and selling utilities.
    V. The pool began operation in 1970, and consists of the state's eight electric utilities.
    The CORRECT answer is:
    A. V, I, II, III, IV
    B. IV, II, I, III, V
    C. III, V, I, IV, II
    D. V, III, IV, II, I

    9.____

10. I. Modern English is much simpler grammatically than Old English.
    II. Finnish grammar is very complicated; there are some fifteen cases, for example.
    III. Chinese, a very old language, may seem to be the exception, but it is the great number of characters/words that must be mastered that makes it so difficult to learn, not its grammar.
    IV. The newest literary language—that is, written as well as spoken—is Finish, whose literary roots go back only to about the middle of the nineteenth century.
    V. Contrary to popular belief, the longer a language is been in use the simpler its grammar—not the reverse.
    The CORRECT answer is:
    A. IV, I, II, III, V
    B. V, I, IV, II, III
    C. I, II, IV, III, V
    D. IV, II, III, I, V

10.____

KEY (CORRECT ANSWERS)

1. D
2. A
3. C
4. D
5. C
6. A
7. C
8. B
9. C
10. B

TEST 2

DIRECTIONS: This type of question tests your ability to recognize accurate paraphrasing, well-constructed paragraphs, and appropriate style and tone. It is important that the answer you select contains only the facts or concepts given in the original sentences. It is also important that you be aware of incomplete sentences, inappropriate transitions, unsupported opinions, incorrect usage, and illogical sentence order. Paragraphs that do not include all the necessary facts and concepts, that distort them, or that add new ones are not considered correct.

The format for this section may vary. Sometimes, long paragraphs are given, and emphasis is placed on style and organization. Our first five questions are of this type. Other times, the paragraphs are shorter, and there is less emphasis on style and more emphasis on accurate representation of information. Our second group of five questions are of this nature.

For each of Questions 1 through 10, select the paragraph that BEST expresses the ideas contained in the sentences above it. *PRINT THE LETTER OF THE CORRECT ANSWER IN THE SPACE AT THE RIGHT.*

1. I. Listening skills are very important for managers.
    II. Listening skills are not usually emphasized.
    III. Whenever managers are depicted in books, manuals or the media, they are always talking, never listening.
    IV. We'd like you to read the enclosed handout on listening skills and to try to consciously apply them this week.
    V. We guarantee they will improve the quality of your interactions.

    A. Unfortunately, listening skills are not usually emphasized for managers. Managers are always depicted as talking, never listening. We'd like you to read the enclosed handout on listening skills. Please try to apply these principles this week. If you do, we guarantee they will improve the quality of your interactions.
    B. The enclosed handout on listening skills will be important improving the quality of your interactions. We guarantee it. All you have to do is take sometime this week to read and to consciously try to apply the principles. Listening skills are very important for manages, but they are not usually emphasized. Whenever managers are depicted in books, manuals or the media, they are always talking, never listening.
    C. Listening well is one of the most important skills a manager can have, yet it's not usually given much attention. Think about any representation of managers in books, manuals, or in the media that you may have seen. They're always talking, never listening. We'd like you to read the enclosed handout on listening skills and consciously try to apply them the rest of the week. We guarantee you will see a difference in the quality of your interactions.

1.____

147

D. Effective listening, one very important tool in the effective manager's arsenal, is usually not emphasized enough. The usual depiction of managers in books, manuals or the media is one in which they are always talking, never listening. We'd like you to read the enclosed handout and consciously try to apply the information contained therein throughout the rest of the week. We feel sure that you will see a marked difference in the quality of your interactions.

2. I. Chekhov wrote three dramatic masterpieces which share certain themes and formats: Uncle Vanya, The Cherry Orchard, and The Three Sisters.
    II. They are primarily concerned with the passage of time and how this erodes human aspirations.
    III. The plays are haunted by the ghosts of the wasted life.
    IV. The characters are concerned with life's lesser problems; however, such as the inability to make decisions, loyalty to the wrong cause, and the inability to be clear.
    V. This results in sweet, almost aching, type of a sadness referred to as Chekhovian.

    2.____

    A. Chekhov wrote three dramatic masterpieces: Uncle Vanya, The Cherry Orchard, and The Three Sisters. These masterpieces share certain themes and formats: the passage of time, how time erodes human aspirations, and the ghosts of wasted life. Each masterpiece is characterized by a sweet, almost aching, type of sadness that has become known as Chekhovian. The sweetness of this sadness hinges on the fact that it is not the great tragedies of life which are destroying these characters, but their minor flaws: indecisiveness, misplaced loyalty, unclarity.
    B. The Cherry Orchard, Uncle Vanya, and The Three Sisters are three dramatic masterpieces written by Chekhov that use similar formats to explore a common theme. Each is primarily concerned with the way that passing time wears down human aspirations, and each is haunted by the ghosts of the wasted life. The characters are shown struggling futilely with the lesser problems of life: indecisiveness, loyalty to the wrong cause, and the inability to be clear. These struggles create a mood of sweet, almost aching, sadness that has become known as Chekhovian.
    C. Chekhov's dramatic masterpieces are, along with The Cherry Orchard, Uncle Vanya, and The Three Sisters. These plays share certain thematic and formal similarities. They are concerned most of all with the passage of time and the way in which time erodes human aspirations. Each play is haunted by the specter of the wasted life. Chekhov's characters are caught, however, by life's lesser snares: indecisiveness, loyalty to the wrong cause, and unclarity. The characteristic mood is a sweet, almost aching type of sadness that has come to be known as Chekhovian.
    D. A Chekhovian mood is characterized by sweet, almost aching, sadness. The term comes from three dramatic tragedies by Chekhov which revolve around the sadness of a wasted life. The three masterpieces (Uncle Vanya, The Three Sisters, and The Cherry Orchard) share the same

theme and format. The plays are concerned with how the passage of time erodes human aspirations. They are peopled with characters who are struggling with life's lesser problems. These are people who are indecisive, loyal to the wrong causes, or are unable to make themselves clear.

3.
I. Movie previews have often helped producers decide which parts of movies they should take out or leave in.
II. The first 1933 preview of King Kong was very helpful to the producers because many people ran screaming from the theater and would not return when four men first attacked by Kong were eaten by giant spiders.
III. The 1950 premiere of Sunset Boulevard resulted in the filming of an entirely new beginning, and a delay of six months in the film's release.
IV. In the original opening scene, William Holden was in a morgue talking with thirty-six other "corpses" about the ways some of them had died.
V. When he began to tell them of his life with Gloria Swanson, the audience found this hilarious, instead of taking the scene seriously.

3.____

A. Movie previews have often helped producers decide what parts of movies they should leave in or take out. For example, the first preview of King Kong in 1933 was very helpful. In one scene, four men were first attacked by Kong and then eaten by giant spiders. Many members of the audience ran screaming from the theater and would not return. The premiere of the 1950 film Sunset Boulevard was also very helpful. In the original opening scene, William Holden was in a morgue with thirty-six other "corpses," discussing the ways some of them had died. When he began to tell them of his life with Gloria Swanson, the audience found this hilarious. They were supposed to take the scene seriously. The result was a delay of six months in the release of the film while a new beginning was added.
B. Movie previews have often helped producers decide whether they should change various parts of a movie. After the 1933 preview of King Kong, a scene in which four men who had been attacked by Kong were eaten by giant spiders was taken out as many people ran screaming from the theater and would not return. The 1950 premiere of Sunset Boulevard also led to some changes. In the original opening scene, William Holden was in a morgue talking with thirty-six other "corpses" about the ways some of them had died. When he began to tell them of his life with Gloria Swanson, the audience found this hilarious, instead of taking the scene seriously.
C. What do Sunset Boulevard and King Kong have in common? Both show the value of using movie previews to test audience reaction. The first 1933 preview of King Kong showed that a scene showing four men being eaten by giant spiders after having been attacked by Kong was too frightening for many people. They ran screaming from the theater and couldn't be coaxed back. The 1950 premiere of Sunset Boulevard was also a scream, but not the kind the producers intended. The movie opens

with William Holden lying in a morgue discussing the ways they had died with thirty-six other "corpses." When he began to tell them of his life with Gloria Swanson, the audience couldn't take him seriously. Their laughter caused a six-month delay while the beginning was rewritten.

    D. Producers very often use movie previews to decide if changes are needed. The premiere of Sunset Boulevard in 1950 led to a new beginning and a six-month delay in film release. At the beginning, William Holden and thirty-six other "corpses" discuss the ways some of them died. Rather than taking this seriously, the audience thought it was hilarious when he began to tell them of his life with Gloria Swanson. The first 1933 preview of King Kong was very helpful for its producers because one scene so terrified the audience that many of them ran screaming from the theater and would not return. In this particular scene, four men who had first been attacked by Kong were eaten by giant spiders.

4.   I. It is common for supervisors to view employees as "things" to be manipulated.   4.____
    II. This approach does not motivate employees, nor does the carrot-and-stick approach because employees often recognize these behaviors and resent them.
    III. Supervisors can change these behaviors by using self-inquiry and persistence.
    IV. The best managers genuinely respect those they work with, are supportive and helpful, and are interested in working as a team with those they supervise.
    V. They disagree with the Golden Rule that says "he or she who has the gold makes the rules."

    A. Some managers act as if they think the Golden Rule means "he or she who has the gold makes the rules." They show disrespect to employees by seeing them as "things" to be manipulated. Obviously, this approach does not motivate employees any more than the carrot-and-stick approach motivates them. The employees are smart enough to spot these behaviors and resent them. On the other hand, the managers genuinely respect those they work with, are supportive and helpful, and are interested in working as a team. Self-inquiry and persistence can change even the former type of supervisor into the latter.
    B. Many supervisors all into the trap of viewing employees as "things" to be manipulated, or try to motivate them by using a carrot-and-stick approach. These methods do not motivate employees, who often recognize the behaviors and resent them. Supervisors can change these behaviors, however, by using self-inquiry and persistence. The best managers are supportive and helpful, and have genuine respect for those with whom they work. They are interested in working as a team with those they supervise. To them, the Golden Rule is not "he or she who has the gold makes the rules."
    C. Some supervisors see employees as "things" to be used or manipulated using a carrot-and-stick technique. These methods don't work. Employees often see through them and resent them. A supervisor who

wants to change may do so. The techniques of self-inquiry and persistence can be used to turn him or her into the type of supervisor who doesn't think the Golden Rule is "he or she who has the gold makes the rules." They may become like the best managers who treat those with whom they work with respect and give them help and support. These are the manager who know how to build a team.

D. Unfortunately, many supervisors act as if their employees are objects whose movements they can position at will. This mistaken belief has the same result as another popular motivational technique—the carrot-and-stick approach. Both attitudes can lead to the same result—resentment from those employees who recognize the behaviors for what they are. Supervisors who recognize these behaviors can change through the use of persistence and the use of self-inquiry. It's important to remember that the best managers respect their employees. They readily give necessary help and support and are interested in working as a team with those they supervise. To these managers, the Golden Rule is not "he or she who has the gold makes the rules."

5.
I. The first half of the nineteenth century produced a group of pessimistic poets—Byron, De Musset, Heine, Pushkin, and Leopardi.
II. It also produced a group of pessimistic composers—Schubert, Chopin, Schumann, and even the later Beethoven.
III. Above all, in philosophy, there was the profoundly pessimistic philosopher, Schopenhauer.
IV. The Revolution was dead, the Bourbons were restored, the feudal barons were reclaiming their land, and progress everywhere was being suppressed, as the great age was over.
V. "I thank God," said Goethe, "that I am not young in so thoroughly finished a world."

   A. "I thank God," said Goethe, "that I am not young in so thoroughly finished a world." The Revolution was dead, the Bourbons were restored, the feudal barons were reclaiming their land, and progress everywhere was being suppressed. The first half of the nineteenth century produced a group of pessimistic poets: Byron, De Musset, Heine, Pushkin, and Leopardi. It also produced pessimistic composers: Schubert, Chopin, Schumann. Although Beethoven came later, he fits into this group, too. Finally and above all, it also produced a profoundly pessimistic philosopher, Schopenhauer. The great age was over.

   B. The first half of the nineteenth century produced a group of pessimistic poets: Byron, De Musset, Heine, Pushkin, and Leopardi. It produced a group of pessimistic composers: Schubert, Chopin, Schumann, and even the later Beethoven. Above all, it produced a profoundly pessimistic philosopher, Schopenhauer. For each of these men, the great age was over. The Revolution was dead, and the Bourbons were restored. The feudal barons were reclaiming their land, and progress everywhere was being suppressed.

C. The great age was over. The Revolution was dead—the Bourbons were restored, and the feudal barons were reclaiming their land. Progress everywhere was being suppressed. Out of this climate came a profound pessimism. Poets, like Byron, De Musset, Heine, Pushkin, and Leopardi; composers, like Schubert, Chopin, Schumann, and even the later Beethoven; and above all, a profoundly pessimistic philosopher, Schopenauer. This pessimism which arose in the first half of the nineteenth century is illustrated by these words of Goethe, "I thank God that I am not young in so thoroughly finished a world."

D. The first half of the nineteenth century produced a group of pessimistic poets, Byron, De Musset, Heine, Pushkin, and Leopardi—and a group of pessimistic composers, Schubert, Chopin, Schumann, and the later Beethoven. Above it all, it produced a profoundly pessimistic philosopher, Schopenhauer. The great age was over. The Revolution was dead, the Bourbons were restored, the feudal barons were reclaiming their land, and progress everywhere was being suppressed. "I thank God," said Goethe, "that I am not young in so thoroughly finished a world."

6. I. A new manager sometimes may feel insecure about his or her competence in the new position.
   II. The new manager may then exhibit defensive or arrogant behavior towards those one supervises, or the new manager may direct overly flattering behavior toward one's new supervisor.

   A. Sometimes, a new manager may feel insecure about his or her ability to perform well in this new position. The insecurity may lead him or her to treat others differently. He or she may display arrogant or defensive behavior towards those he or she supervises, or be overly flattering to his or her new supervisor.
   B. A new manager may sometimes feel insecure about his or her ability to perform well in the new position. He or she may then become arrogant, defensive, or overly flattering towards those he or she works with.
   C. There are times when a new manager may be insecure about how well he or she can perform in the new job. The new manager may also behave defensive or act in an arrogant way towards those he or she supervises, or overly flatter his or her boss.
   D. Sometimes a new manager may feel insecure about his or her ability to perform well in the new position. He or she may then display arrogant or defensive behavior towards those they supervise, or become overly flattering towards their supervisors.

6.____

7. I. It is possible to eliminate unwanted behavior by bringing it under stimulus control—tying the behavior to a cue, and then never, or rarely, giving the cue.
   II. One trainer successfully used this method to keep an energetic young porpoise from coming out of her tank whenever she felt like it, which was potentially dangerous.
   III. Her trainer taught her to do it for a reward, in response to a hand signal, and then rarely gave the signal.

7.____

A. Unwanted behavior can be eliminated by tying the behavior to a cue, and then never, or rarely, giving the cue. This is called stimulus control. One trainer was able to use this method to keep an energetic young porpoise from coming out of her tank by teaching her to come out for a reward in response to a hand signal, and then rarely giving the signal.

B. Stimulus control can be used to eliminate unwanted behavior. In this method, behavior is tied to a cue, and then the cue is rarely, if ever, given. One trainer was able to successfully use stimulus control to keep an energetic young porpoise from coming out of her tank whenever she felt like it—a potentially dangerous practice. She taught the porpoise to come out for a reward when she gave a hand signal, and then rarely gave the signal.

C. It is possible to eliminate behavior that is undesirable by bringing it under stimulus control by tying behavior to a signal, and then rarely giving the signal. One trainer successfully used this method to keep an energetic porpoise from coming out of her tank, a potentially dangerous situation. Her trainer taught the porpoise to do it for a reward, in response to a hand signal, and then would rarely give the signal.

D. By using stimulus control, it is possible to eliminate unwanted behavior by tying the behavior to a cue, and then rarely or never give the cue. One trainer was able to use this method to successfully stop a young porpoise from coming out of her tank whenever she felt like it. To curb this potentially dangerous practice, the porpoise was taught by the trainer to come out of the tank for a reward, in response to a hand signal, and then rarely given the signal.

8. I. There is a great deal of concern over the safety of commercial trucks, caused by their greatly increased role in serious accidents since federal deregulation in 1981.
    II. Recently, 60 percent of trucks in New York and Connecticut and 70 percent of trucks in Maryland randomly stopped by state troopers failed safety inspections.
    III. Sixteen states in the United States require no training at all for truck drivers.

    A. Since federal deregulation in 1981, there has been a great deal of concern over the safety of commercial trucks, and their greatly increased role in serious accidents. Recently, 60 percent of trucks in New York and Connecticut, and 70 percent of trucks in Maryland failed safety inspections. Sixteen states in the United States require no training at all for truck drivers.

    B. There is a great deal of concern over the safety of commercial trucks since federal deregulation in 1981. Their role in serious accidents has greatly increased. Recently, 60 percent of trucks randomly stopped in Connecticut and New York and 70 percent in Maryland failed safety inspections conducted by state troopers. Sixteen states in the United States provide no training at all for truck drivers.

    C. Commercial trucks have a greatly increased role in serious accidents since federal deregulation in 1981. This has led to a great deal of concern.

Recently, 70 percent of trucks in Maryland and 60 percent of trucks in New York and Connecticut failed inspection of those that were randomly stopped by state troopers. Sixteen states in the United States require no training for all truck drivers.

D. Since federal deregulation in 1981, the role that commercial trucks have played in serious accidents has greatly increased, and this has led to a great deal of concern. Recently, 60 percent of trucks in New York and Connecticut, and 70 percent of trucks in Maryland randomly stopped by state troopers failed safety inspections. Sixteen states in the U.S. don't require any training for truck drivers.

9. I. No matter how much some people have, they still feel unsatisfied and want more, or want to keep what they have forever.
    II. One recent television documentary showed several people flying from New York to Paris for a one-day shopping spree to buy platinum earrings, because they were bored.
    III. In Brazil, some people were ordering coffins that cost a minimum of $45,000 and are equipping them with deluxe stereos, televisions, and other graveyard necessities.

    A. Some people, despite having a great deal, still feel unsatisfied and want more, or think they can keep what they have forever. One recent documentary on television showed several people enroute from Paris to New York for a one day shopping spree to buy platinum earrings, because they were bored. Some people in Brazil are even ordering coffins equipped with such graveyard necessities as deluxe stereos and televisions. The price of the coffins start at $45,000.
    B. No matter how much some people have, they may feel unsatisfied. This leads them to want more, or to want to keep what they have forever. Recently, a television documentary depicting several people flying from New York to Paris for a one day shopping spree to buy platinum earrings. They were bored. Some people in Brazil are ordering coffins that cost at least $45,000 and come equipped with deluxe televisions, stereos and other necessary graveyard items.
    C. Some people will be dissatisfied no matter how much they have. They may want more, or they may want to keep what they have forever. One recent television documentary showed several people, motivated by boredom, jetting from New York to Paris for a one-day shopping spree to buy platinum earrings. In Brazil, some people are ordering coffins equipped with deluxe stereos, televisions and other graveyard necessities. The minimum price for these coffins—$45,000.
    D. Some people are never satisfied. No matter how much they have they still want more, or think they can keep what they have forever. One television documentary recently showed several people flying from New York to Paris for the day to buy platinum earrings because they were bored. In Brazil, some people are ordering coffins that cost $45,000 and are equipped with deluxe stereos, televisions and other graveyard necessities.

9.____

10.
I. A television signal or video signal has three parts.
II. Its parts are the black-and-white portion, the color portion, and the synchronizing (sync) pulses, which keep the picture stable.
III. Each video source, whether it's a camera or a video-cassette recorder contains its own generator of these synchronizing pulses to accompany the picture that it's sending in order to keep it steady and straight.
IV. In order to produce a clean recording, a video-cassette recorder must "lock-up" to the sync pulses that are part of the video it is trying to record, and this effort may be very noticeable if the device does not have gunlock.

10._____

A. There are three parts to a television or video signal: the black-and-white part, the color part, and the synchronizing (sync) pulses, which keep the picture stable. Whether it's a video-cassette recorder or a camera, each video source contains its own pulse that synchronizes and generates the picture it's sending in order to keep it straight and steady. A video-cassette recorder must "lock up" to the sync pulses that are part of the video it's trying to record. If the device doesn't have gunlock, this effort must be very noticeable.
B. A video signal or television is comprised of three parts: the black-and-white portion, the color portion, and the sync (synchronizing) pulses, which keep the picture stable. Whether it's a camera or a video-cassette recorder, each video source contains its own generator of these synchronizing pulses. These accompany the picture that it's sending in order to keep it straight and steady. A video-cassette recorder must "lock up" to the sync pulses that are part of the video it is trying to record in order to produce a clean recording. This effort may be very noticeable if the device does not have gunlock.
C. There are three parts to a television or video signal: the color portion, the black-and-white portion, and the sync (synchronizing pulses). These keep the picture stable. Each video source, whether it's a video-cassette recorder or a camera, generates these synchronizing pulses accompanying the picture it's sending in order to keep it straight and steady. If a clean recording is to be produced, a video-cassette recorder must store the sync pulses that are part of the video it is trying to record. This effort may not be noticeable if the device does not have gunlock.
D. A television signal or video signal has three parts: the black-and-white portion, the color portion, and the synchronizing (sync) pulses. It's the sync pulses which keep the picture stable, which accompany it and keep it steady and straight. Whether it's a camera or a video-cassette recorder, each video source contains its own generator of these synchronizing pulses. To produce a clean recording, a video-cassette recorder must "lock up" to the sync pulses that are part of the video it is trying to record. If the device does not have gunlock, this effort may be very noticeable.

KEY (CORRECT ANSWERS)

1.	C	6.	A
2.	B	7.	B
3.	A	8.	D
4.	B	9.	C
5.	D	10.	D

BASIC FUNDAMENTALS OF WRITTEN COMMUNICATION

CONTENTS	Page
INSTRUCTIONAL OBJECTIVES	1
CONTENT	1
Introduction	1
1. Business Writing	1
Letters	
Selet the letter type	
Select the Right Format	
Know the Letter Elements	
Be Breef	
Use Concrete Nouns	
Use Active Verbs	
Use a Natural Tone	
Forms	4
Memoranda	5
Minutes of meetings	5
Short Reports	6
News Releases	8
2. Reporting on a Topic	9
Preparation for the Report	9
What is the Purpose of the Report?	
What Questions Should it Answer?	
Where Can the Relevant information be obtained?	
The Text of the Report	10
What Are the Answers to the Questions?	
Organizing the Report	
The Writer's Responsibilities	11
Conclusions and Recommendations	11
3. Persuasive Writing	11
General Guidelines for Writing	11
Persuasively	
Know the Source Credibility	
Avoid Overemotional Appeal	
Consider the Other Man's Point of wiew	
Interpersonal Communications	12
Conditions of Persuading	
The Persuassion campain	
4. Instructional Writing	13
Advances Organizers	
Practice	
Errorless Learning	
Feedback	
STUDENT LEARNING ACTIVITIES	16
TEACHERS MANAGEMENT ACTIVTIES	17
EVALUATION QUESTIONS	19

BASIC FUNDAMENTALS OF WRITTEN COMMUNICATION

INSTRUCTIONAL OBJECTIVES

1. Ability to write legibly.
2. Ability to fill out forms and applications correctly.
3. Ability to take messages and notes accurately.
4. Ability to write letters effectively.
5. Ability to write directions and instructions clearly.
6. Ability to outline written and spoken information.
7. Ability to persuade or teach others through written communication.
8. Ability to write effective overviews and summaries.
9. Ability to make smooth transitions within written communications.
10. Ability to use language forms appropriate for the reader.
11. Ability to prepare effective informational reports.

CONTENT

INTRODUCTION

Public-service employees are required to prepare written communications for a variety of purposes. Written communication is a fundamental tool, not only for the public-service occupations, but throughout the world of work. Many public-service occupations require written communication with ordinary citizens of diverse backgrounds, so the trainee should develop the ability to write in simple, nontechnical language that the ordinary citizen will understand.

This unit is designed to develop the student's ability to communicate effectively in writing for a number of different purposes and in a number of different formats. Whatever the particular purpose or format, however, effective writing will require the writer:

- to have a clear idea of his purpose and his audience;
- to organize his thoughts and information in an orderly way;
- to express himself concisely, accurately, and concretely;
- to report relevant facts;
- to explain and summarize ideas clearly; and
- to evaluate the effectiveness of his communication.

1. BUSINESS WRITING

   Several forms of written communication tend to recur frequently in most public-service agencies, including:
   - letters
   - forms
   - memoranda
   - minutes of meetings
   - short reports
   - telegrams and cables
   - news releases
   - and many others

   The public-service employee should be familiar with the principles of writing in these forms, and should be able to apply them in preparing effective communications.

   Letters

   Every letter sent from a public-service agency should be considered an ambassador of goodwill. The impression it creates may mean the difference between favorable public attitudes or unfavorable ones. It may mean the difference between creating a friend or an enemy for the agency. Every public-service employee has a responsibility to serve the public effectively and to provide services in an efficient and courteous manner. The letters an agency sends out reflect its attitudes toward the public.

The impression a letter creates depends upon both its appearance and its tone. A letter which shows erasures and pen written corrections gives an impression that the sending agency is slovenly. Similarly, a rude or impersonal letter creates the impression that the agency is insensitive or unfeeling. In preparing letters, the employee should apply principles of style and tone which will serve to create the most favorable impression.

Select the Letter Type. The two most common types of business letters are letters of inquiry and letters of response - that is, "asking" letters and "answering" letters. Whichever type of letter the employee is asked to write, the following guidelines will simplify the task and help to achieve a style and tone which will create a favorable impression on the reader.

Select the Right Format. Several styles of letter format are in common use today, including:

- the indented format,
- the block format, and
- the semi-block format.

Modified forms of these are also in use in some offices. The student should become familiar with the formats preferred for usage in his office, and be able to use whichever form the employer requests.

Know the Letter Elements. Every letter includes certain basic elements, such as:

- the letterhead, which identifies the name and address of the sender.
- the date on which the letter was transmitted.
- the inside address, with the name, street, city, and state of the addressee.
- the salutation, greeting the addressee.
- the body, containing the message.
- the complimentary close, the "good-bye" of the business letter.
- the signature, handwritten by the sender.
- the typed signature, the typewritten name and title of the sender.

In addition, several other elements are occasionally found in business letters:

- the *attention line,* directing the letter to the attention of a particular individual or his representative.
- the *subject line,* informing the reader at a glance of the subject of the letter.

- the *enclosure notation,* noting items enclosed with the letter.
- the *copy notation,* listing other persons who receive copies of the letter.
- the *postscript,* an afterthought sometimes (but not normally) added following the last typed line of the letter.

Be *Brief.* Use only the words which help to say what is needed in a clear and straightforward manner. Do not repeat information already known to the reader, or contained elsewhere in the letter. Likewise, do not repeat information contained in the letter being answered. Rather than repeat the content of a previous letter, one can say something like, "Please refer to our letter dated March 5:"

An employee can shorten his letters by using single words that serve the same function as longer phrases. Many commonly used phrases can be replaced by single words. For example,

Phrase	Single word
in order to	to
in reference to in	about
the amount of	for, of
in a number of cases	some
in view of	because
with regard to	about, in

Similarly, avoid the use of adjectives and nouns that are formed from verbs. If the root verbs are used instead, the writing will be more concise and more vivid. For example,

Noun form	Verb form
We made an adjustment on our books	We adjusted our books
We are sorry we cannot make a replacement of	We are sorry we cannot replace
Please make a correction in our order	Please correct our order

Be on the lookout for unnecessary adjectives and adverbs which tend to clutter letters without adding information or improving style. Such unnecessary words tend to distract the reader and make it more difficult for him to grasp the main points. Observe how the superfluous words, italicized in the following example, obscure the meaning: "You may be *very much* disappointed to learn that the *excessively large* demand for our *highly popular recent* publication, 'Your Income Taxes,' has led to an *unexpected* shortage of this *attractive* publication and we *sadly* expect they will not be replenished until *quite* late this year."

Summarizing, then, a *good letter is simple and clear, with short, simple words, sentences, and paragraphs. Related parts* of *sentences and paragraphs are kept together and placed in an order which makes it easy for the reader to follow the main thoughts.*

Be Natural. Whenever possible, use a human touch. Use names and personal pronouns to let the reader know the letter was written by a person, not an institution. Instead of saying, "It is the policy of this agency to contact its clients once each year to confirm their status," try this: "Our policy, Mr. Jones, is to confirm your status once each year."

Use Concrete Nouns. Avoid using abstract words and generalizations. Use names of objects, places, and persons rather than abstractions.

Use Active verbs. The passive voice gives a motionless, weak tone to most writing. Instead of "The minutes were taken by Mrs. Smith," say, "Mrs. Smith took the minutes." Instead of "The plans were prepared by the banquet committee," say, "The banquet committee prepared the plans."

Use a Natural Tone. Many people tend to become hard, cold, and unnatural the moment they write a letter. *Communicating by letter should have the same natural tone of conversation used in everyday speech.* One way to achieve a natural and personal tone in the majority of letters is through the use of personal pronouns. Instead of saying, "Referring to your letter of March 5, reporting the non-receipt of goods ordered last February 15, please be advised that the goods were shipped as requested," say, "I am sorry to hear that you failed to receive the items you ordered last February 15. We shipped them the same day we received your letter."

Forms

In most businesses and public service agencies, repetitive work is simplified by the use of *forms*. Forms exist for nearly every purpose imaginable: for ordering supplies, preparing invoices, applying for jobs, applying for insurance, paying taxes, recording inventories, and so on. While the forms encountered in different agencies may differ widely, several principles should be applied in completing any form:

- *Legibility.* Entries on forms should be clear and legible. Print or type wherever possible. When space provided is insufficient, attach a supplementary sheet to the form.

- *Completeness.* Make an entry in every space provided on the form. If a particular space does not apply to the applicant, enter there the term "N/A" (for "not applicable"). The reader of the completed form will then know that the applicant did not simply overlook that space.

- *Conciseness.* Forms are intended to elicit a maximum amount of information in the least possible space. When completing a form, it is usually not necessary to write complete sentences. Provide the necessary information in the least possible words.

- *Accuracy.* Be sure the information provided on the form is accurate. If the entry is a number, such as a social security number or an address, double-check the correctness of the number. Be sure of the spelling of names, No one appreciates receiving a communication in which his name is misspelled.

Memoranda

The written communications passing between offices or departments are usually transmitted in a form known as *"interoffice memorandum."* The headings most often used on such "memos" are:

- TO: identifying the addressee,
- FROM: identifying the sender or the originating office,
- SUBJECT: identifying briefly the subject of the memo,
- DATE: identifying the date the memo was prepared.

Larger agencies may also use headings such as FILE or REFERENCE NO. to aid in filing and retrieving memoranda.

In writing a memo, many of the same rules for letter-writing may be applied. Both the appearance and tone of the memo should create a pleasing impression. The format should be neat and follow the standards set by the originating office. The tone should be friendly, courteous, and considerate. The language should be clear, concise, and complete.

Memos usually dispense with salutations, complimentary closings, and signatures of the writers. In most other respects, however, the memorandum will follow the rules of good letter-writing.

Minutes of Meetings

Most formal public-service organization conduct meetings from time to time at which group decisions are made about agency policies, procedures, and work assignments. The records of such meetings are called *minutes.*

Minutes should be written as clearly and simply as possible, summarizing only the essential facts and decisions made at the meeting. While some issue may have been discussed at great length, only the final decision or resolution made of it should be recorded in the minutes. Information of this sort is usually included:

- Time and place of the call to order,
- Presiding officer and secretary,
- Voting members present (with names, if a small organization),

- Approval and corrections of previous minutes,
- Urgent business,
- Old business,
- New business,
- Time of adjournment,
- Signature of recorder.

Minutes should be written in a factual and objective style. The opinions of the recorder should not be in evidence. Every item of business coming up before a meeting should be included in the minutes, together with its disposition. For example:

- "M/S/P (Moved, seconded, passed) that Mr. Thomas Jones take responsibility for rewriting the personnel procedures manual."
- "Discussion of the summer vacation schedule was tabled until the next meeting."
- "M/S/P, a resolution that no client of the agency should be kept waiting more than 20 minutes for an interview."

Note that considerable discussion may have surrounded each of the above items in the minutes, but that only the topic and its resolution are recorded.

Short Reports

The public-service employee often is called upon to prepare a short report gathering and interpreting information on a single topic. Reports of this kind are sometimes prepared so that all the relevant information may be assembled in one place to aid the organization in making certain decisions. Such reports may be read primarily by the staff of the organization or by others closely related to the decision-making process.

Reports may be prepared at other times for distribution to the public or to other agencies and institutions. These reports may serve the purpose of informing public opinion or persuading others on matters of public policy.

Whatever the purpose of the short report, its physical appearance and style of presentation should be designed to create a favorable impression on the reader. Even if the report is distributed only within the writer's own unit, an attractive, clear, thorough report will reflect the writer's dedication to his assignment and the pride he takes in his work.

Some guidelines which will assist the trainee in preparation of effective short reports include use of the following:

- A good quality paper;
- Wide and even margins, allowing binding room;

- An accepted standard style of typing;
- A title page;
- A table of contents (for more lengthy reports only);
- A graphic numbering or outlining system, if needed for clarity;
- Graphics and photos to clarify meaning when useful;
- Footnotes, used sparingly, and only when they contribute to the report;
- A bibliography of sources, using a standard citation style.

A discussion of the organization of content for informational reports follows later in this document.

News Releases

From time to time, the public-service employees may be called upon to prepare a news release for his agency. Whenever the activities of the agency are newsworthy or of interest to the public, the agency has an obligation to report such activities to the press. The most common means for such reporting is by using the press release. Most newspapers and broadcasting stations are initially informed of agencies' activities by news releases distributed by the agencies themselves. Thus, the news release is a basic tool for communicating with the public served by the agency.

The news release is written in news style, with these basic characteristics:

- Sentences are short and simple.

- Paragraphs are short (one or two sentences) and relate to a single item of information.

- Paragraphs are arranged in *inverted order* — the most important in information appears first.

- The first or *lead* paragraph summarizes the entire story. If the reader went no further, he would have the essential information.

- Subsequent paragraphs provide further details, the most important occurring first.

- Reported information is attributed to sources; that is, the source of the news is reported in the story.

- The expression of the writer's opinions is scrupulously avoided.

- The 5 W's (who, what, why, where, when) are included.

News releases should be typed double spaced on standard 8 1/2 x 11 paper, with generous margins and at least 2" of open space above the lead paragraph. Do not write headlines - that is the editor's job. At the top of the first page of the release include the name of the agency releasing the story and the name and phone number of the person to contact if more information is needed. If the release runs more than one page, end each page with the word "-more-" to indicate that more copy follows. End the release with the symbols "###" to indicate that the copy ends at that point.

Accuracy and physical appearance are essential characteristics of the news release. Typographical errors, or errors of fact, such as misspelled names, lead editors to doubt the reliability of the story. Great care should be taken to assure the accuracy and reliability of a news release.

2. REPORTING ON A TOPIC

At one time or another, most public-service employees will be asked to prepare a report on some topic. Usually the need for the report grows out of some policy decision contemplated by the agency for which full information must be considered. For example:

- Should the agency undertake some new project or service?
- Should working conditions be changed?
- Are new specialists needed on the staff?
- Or should a branch office be opened up?

Or any of a hundred other such decisions which the agency must make from time to time.

When called upon to prepare such a report, the employee should have a model to follow which will guide his collection of information and will help him to prepare an effective and useful report.

As with other forms of written communication, both the physical appearance and content of the report are important to create a favorable impression and to engender confidence. The physical appearance of such reports has been discussed earlier; additional suggestions for reports are given in Unit 3. Basic guidelines follow below for organizing and preparing the content.

Preparation for the Report

What is the Purpose of the Report? The preparer of the report should have clearly in mind why the report is needed:

- What is the decision being contemplated by the agency?
- To what use will the report be put?

Before beginning to prepare the report, the writer should discuss its purpose fully with the decision-making staff to articulate the purpose the report is intended to serve. If the employee is himself initiating the report, it would be well to discuss its purpose with colleagues to assure that its purpose is clear in his own mind.

What Questions Should the Report Answer? Once the purpose of the report is clear, the questions the report must answer may begin to become clear. For example, if the decision faced by the agency is whether or not to offer a new service, questions may be asked such as these:

- What persons would be served by the new service?

- What would the new service cost?
- What new staff would be needed?
- What new equipment and facilities would be needed?
- What alternative ways exist for offering the service?
- How might the new service be administered?

And so on. Unless the purpose of the report is clear, it is difficult to decide what specific questions need to be answered. Once the purpose is clear, these questions can be specified.

Where Can the Relevant Information be Obtained? Once the questions are clear in the writer's mind, he can identify the information he will need to answer them. Information may usually be obtained from two general sources:

- *Relevant documents.* Records, publications, and other reports are often useful in locating the information needed to answer particular questions. These may be in the files of the writer's own agency, in other agencies, or in libraries.

- *Personal contacts.* Persons in a position to know the needed information may be contacted in person, by phone, or by letter. Such contacts are especially important in obtaining firsthand accounts of previous experience.

The Text of the Report

What are the Answers to the Questions? Once the relevant information is in hand, the answers to the questions may be assembled.

- What does the information reveal? This activity amounts to summarizing the information obtained. It often helps to organize this summary around the specific questions asked by the report. For example, if the report asks in one part, "What are the costs of the new service likely to be?" one section of the report should summarize the information gathered to answer this question.

Organizing the Report. The organization of a report into main and subsections depends upon the nature of the report. Reports will differ widely in their organization and treatment. In general, however, the report should generally follow the pattern previously discussed. That is, reports which generally include the following subjects in order will be found to be clear in their intent and to communicate effectively:

- *Description of problem or purpose.* Example: "One problem facing our agency is whether or not we should extend our hours of operation to better serve the public. This report is intended to examine the problem and make recommendations."

- *Questions to be answered.* Example: "In examining this problem, answers were sought to the following questions: What persons would be served? What would it cost? What staff would be needed?"

- *Information sources.* Example: "To answer these questions, letters of complaint for the past three years were examined. Interviews with clients were conducted by phone and in person, phone interviews were conducted with the agency directors in Memphis, Philadelphia, and Chicago."

- *Summary of findings.* Example: "At least 25 percent of the agency's clients would be served better by evening or Saturday service. The costs of operating eight hours of extended service would be negligible, since the service could be provided by rescheduling work assignments. The present staff report they would be inconvenienced by evening and Saturday work assignments."

<u>The Writer's Responsibilities.</u> It is the writer's responsibility to address finally the original purpose of the report. Once the questions have been answered, an informed judgment can be made as to the decision facing the agency. It is at this stage that the writer attempts to draw conclusions from the information he has gathered and summarized. For example, if the original purpose of the report was to help make a decision about whether or not the agency should offer a new service, the writer should draw conclusions from the information and recommend either for or against the new service.

<u>Conclusions and Recommendations.</u> Example: "It appears that operating during extended hours would better serve a significant number of clients. The writer recommends that the agency offer this new service. The present staff should be given temporary assignments to cover the extended hours. As new staff are hired to replace separating persons, they should be hired specifically to cover the extended hours."

3. **PERSUASIVE WRITING**

   Often in life, people are called upon to persuade individuals and groups to adopt ideas believed to be good, or attitudes favorable to ideas thought to be worthwhile or behavior believed to be beneficial. The public service employee may find he must persuade the staff of his own agency, his superiors, the clients of the agency, or the general public in his community.

   Persuading others by means of written and other forms of communication is a difficult task and requires much practice. Some principles have emerged from the study of persuasion which may provide some guidelines for developing a model for persuasive writing.

General Guidelines for Writing Persuasively

Know the Credibility of the Source. People are more likely to be persuaded by a message they perceive originates from a trustworthy source. Their trust is enhanced if the source is seen as authoritative, or knowledgeable on the issue discussed in the message. Their trust is increased also if the source appears to have nothing to gain either way, has no vested interest in the final decision. Then, the assertions made in persuasive writing should be backed up by referencing trustworthy and disinterested information sources.

Avoid Overemotional Appeals. Appealing to the common emotions of man—love, hate, tear, sex, etc.—can have a favorable effect on the outcome of a persuasive message. But care should be taken because, if the appeal is too strong, it can lead to a reverse effect. For example, if an agency wanted to persuade the public to get chest X-rays, it would have much greater chance of success if it adopted a positive and helpful attitude rather than trying to frighten them into this action. For instance, appealing mildly to the sense of well-being which accompanies knowledge of one's own good health, instead of shocking the public by showing horror pictures of patients who died from lack of timely X-rays.

Consider the Other Man's Point of View. To persuade another to one's own point of view, should the writer include information and arguments contrary to his own position? Or should he argue only for his own side?

Generally, it depends on where most of the audience stand in the first place. If most of the audience already favor the position being advocated, then the writer will probably do better including only information favorable to his position. However, if the greater part of the audience are likely to oppose this position, then the writer would probably be better off including their arguments also. In this case, he may be helping his cause by rebutting the opposing arguments as he introduces them into the writing.

An example of this technique might occur in arguing for such an idea as a four-day, forty-hour workweek. Thus: "Many people feel that the ten-hour day is too long and that they would arrive home too late for their regular dinner hour. But think! If you have dinner a littler later each night, you'll have a three-day weekend every week. More days free to go fishing, or camping. More days with your wife and children." That is good persuasive writing!

Interpersonal Communications

The important role of interpersonal communication in persuading others—face-to-face and person-to-person communications—has been well documented. Mass mailings or printed messages will likely have less effect than personal letters and conversations between persons already known to each other. In any persuasion campaign the personal touch is very important.

An individual in persuading a large number of persons will likely be more effective if he can organize a letter-writing campaign of persuasive messages written by persons favorable to his position to their friends and acquaintances, than if his campaign is based upon sending out a mass mailing of a printed message.

Conditions for Persuading. In order for an audience of one or many to be persuaded in the manner desired, these conditions must be met:

- the audience must be *exposed* to the message,
- members of the audience must *perceive* the intent of the message,
- they must *remember* the message afterwards,
- each member must *decide* whether or not to adopt the ideas.

Each member of the audience will respond to a message differently. While every person may receive the message, not everyone will read it. Even among those who read it, not everyone will perceive it in the same way. Some will remember it longer than others. Not everyone will decide to adopt the ideas. These effects are called *selective exposure, selective perception, selective retention,* and *selective decision.*

The Persuasion Campaign. How can one counteract these selective effects in persuading others? One thing that is known is that *people tend to be influenced by persuasive messages which they are already predisposed to accept.* This means a person is more likely to persuade people a little than to persuade them a lot.

In planning a persuasion campaign, therefore, the messages should be tailored to the audiences. Success will be more likely if one starts with people who believe *almost* as the writer wants to persuade them to believe—people who are most likely to agree with the position advocated.

The writer also wants to use arguments based on values the particular audience already accepts. For example, in advocating a new teen-age job program, he might argue with business men that the program will help business; with parents, that it will build character; with teachers, that it is educational; with taxpayers, that it will reduce future taxes; and so on.

The idea is to find some way to make sure that each member of the particular audiences reached can see an advantage for himself, and for the writer to then tailor the messages for those audiences.

4. INSTRUCTIONAL WRITING

Another task that the public-service employee may expect to face from time to time is the instruction of some other person in the performance of a task. This may sometimes involve preparing written instructions to other employees in the unit, or preparing a training manual for new employees.

It may sometimes involve preparing instructional manuals for clients of the unit, such as "How to Apply for a Real Estate License," "How to Bathe your Baby," or "How to Recognize the Symptoms of Heart Disease."

Whatever the purpose or the audience, certain principles of instruction may be applied which will help make more effective these instructional or training communications. These are: *advance organizers, practice, errorless learning,* and *feedback*.

Advance Organizers

At or near the beginning of an instructional communication, it helps the learner if he is provided with what can be called an "advance organizer." This element of the communication performs two functions:

- it provides a framework or "map" for the leader to organize the information he will encounter,
- it helps the learner perceive his purpose in learning the tasks which will follow.

The first paragraphs in this section, for example, serve together as an advance organizer. The trainee is informed that he may be called upon to perform these tasks in his job *(perceived purpose),* and that he will be instructed in advance organizers, practice, errorless learning, and feedback *(framework, or "map")*.

Practice

The notion of *practice makes perfect* is a sound instructional principle. When trying to teach someone to perform a task by means of written communication, the writer should build in many opportunities for practicing the task, or parts of it. This built-in practice should be both appropriate and active:

- *Appropriate practice* is practice which is directly related to learning the tasks at hand.

- *Active practice* is practice in actually performing the task at hand or parts of it, rather than simply reading about the task, or thinking about it.

By inserting questions into the text of the communication, by giving practice quizzes, exercises, or field work, one can build into his instructional communication the kind of practice necessary for the reader to readily learn the task.

Errorless Learning

The practice given learners should be easy to do. That is, they should not be asked to practice a task if they are likely to make a lot of mistakes. When a mistake is practiced it is likely to recur again and again, like spelling "demons," which have been spelled wrong so often it's difficult to recall the way they should be spelled. Because it is better to practice a task right from the first, it is important that learners do not make errors in practice.

- One method for encouraging correct practice is to give the reader hints, or *prompts,* to help him practice correctly.

- Another method is to instruct him in a logical sequence a little bit at a time. Don't try to teach everything at once. Break the task down into small parts and teach each part of the task in order. Then give the learner practice in each part of the task before giving him practice in the whole thing.

- A third way of encouraging errorless learning is to build in practice and review throughout the communication. The learner may forget part of the task if the teacher doesn't review it with him from time to time.

Remember, people primarily learn from what they do, so build in to the instructional communication many opportunities for the learner to practice correctly all of the parts of the task required for learning, first separately and then all together.

Feedback

The reader, or learner, can't judge how well he is learning the task unless he is informed of it. In a classroom situation, the teacher usually confirms that the learner has been successful, or points out the errors he made, and provides additional instruction. An instructional communication can also help learners in the same way, by providing *feedback* to the learner.

Following practice, the writer should include in his instructional communication information which will let the reader know whether he performed the task correctly. In case he didn't, the writer should also include some further information which will help the reader perform it correctly next time. This feedback, then, performs two functions:

- it helps the learner confirm that his practice was done correctly, and

- it helps him correct his performance of the task in case he made any errors.

Feedback will be most helpful to the learner if it occurs immediately following practice. The learner should be brought to know of his success or his errors just as soon as possible after practice.

STUDENT LEARNING ACTIVITIES

- Write "asking" and "answering" letters, and answer a letter of complaint, using the format assigned by the teacher.

- Write memoranda to other "offices" in a fictitious organization. Plan a field trip using only memos to communicate with other students in the class.

- Take minutes of a small group meeting. Or attend a meeting of the school board and take minutes.

- Write a short report on a public service occupation of special interest to you.

- Write a 15-word telegram reserving a single room at a hotel and asking to be picked up at the airport.

- Write a news release announcing a new service offered to the public by your agency.

- Based upon hearing a reading or pretaping of a report, summarize the report in news style.

- View films on effective communication, for example, *Getting the Facts, Words that Don't Inform,* and *A Message to No One.*

- For a given problem or purpose, compile a list of specific questions you would need to answer to write a report on the topic.

- For a given list of questions, discuss and compile a list of information sources relevant to the questions.

- As a member of a group, consider the problem of "What field trip should the class take to help students learn how to write an effective news release?" What questions will you need to answer? Where will you obtain your information?

- As a member of a group, gather the information and prepare a short report based on it for presentation to the class.

- Write a report on a problem assigned by your teacher.

- Write a brief persuasive letter to a friend on a given topic. Assume he does not already agree with you. Apply principles of source credibility, emotional appeals, and one or both sides of the issue to persuade him.

- Plan a persuasive campaign to persuade a given segment of your community to take some given action.

- Write a short instructional communication on a verbal learning task assigned by your teacher.

- Write a short instructional communication on a learning task which involves the operation of equipment.

- Try your instructional communications with a fellow student to check for errors during practice.

TEACHER MANAGEMENT ACTIVITIES

- Have students practice letter writing. Assign letters of "asking" and "answering." Read them a letter of complaint and ask them to write an answering letter. Establish common rules of format and style for each assignment. Change the rules from time to time to give practice in several styles.

- Have small groups plan an event, such as a field trip, assigning the various tasks to one another using only memoranda. Evaluate the effectiveness of each group's memo writing by the speed and completeness of their planning.

- Have the class attend a public meeting. Assign each the task of taking the minutes. Evaluate the minutes for brevity and completeness.

- Encourage each student to prepare a short report on a public service occupation of special interest to himself.

- Give the students practice in writing 15-word telegrams.

- Have the students prepare a news release announcing some new service offered to the public, such as "Taxpayers can now obtain help from the Internal Revenue Service in completing their income tax forms as a result of a new service now being offered by the agency."

- Give the students practice in summarizing and writing leads by giving them the facts of a news event and asking them to write a one or two-sentence lead summarizing the significant facts of the event.

- Read a speech or a story. Have students write a summary and a report of the speech or story in news style.

- Show films on effective communication, for example, *Getting the Facts, Words that Don't Inform,* and *A Message to No One.*

- State a general problem and have each student prepare a list of the specific questions implied by the problem.

- State a list of specific questions and discuss with the class the sources of information which might bear upon each of the questions.

- Have small groups consider and write short reports jointly on the general problem, "What field trip should the class take to help students learn how to write an effective news release?" Have each group identify the specific questions to be answered, with sources for needed information.

- Have each student identify and prepare a short report on a general problem of interest.

- Assign students to work in groups of three or four to draft a letter to a friend to persuade him to make a contribution to establish a new city art museum.

- Assign the students to groups of five or six, each group to map out a persuasive campaign on a given topic. Some topics are "Give Blood," "Get Chest X-Ray," "Quit Smoking," "Don't Litter," "Inspect Your House Wiring," etc.

- Have each student identify a simple verbal learning task and prepare an instructional communication to teach that task to another student not familiar with the task.

- Have each student prepare an instructional manual designed to train someone to operate some simple piece of equipment, such as an adding machine, a slide projector, a tape recorder, or something of similar complexity.

- Have each student try his instructional communication out on another student, unfamiliar with the task. He should observe the activities and responses of the trial student to identify errors made in practice. He should revise the communication, adding practice, review, and prompts wherever needed to reduce errors in practice.

EVALUATION QUESTIONS

Written Communications

1. Which type of letter would be correct for a public service worker to send?

    A. A letter containing erasures
    B. A letter reflecting goodwill
    C. A rude letter
    D. An impersonal letter

    1.____

2. Memos usually leave out:

    A. Complimentary closings
    B. The name of the sender
    C. The name of the addressee
    D. The date the memo was sent

    2.____

3. A good business letter would not contain:

    A. Short, simple words, sentences, and paragraphs
    B. Information contained in the letter being answered
    C. Concrete nouns and active verbs
    D. Orderly placed paragraphs

    3.____

4. In writing business letters it is important to:

    A. Use a conversational tone
    B. Use a hard, cold tone
    C. Use abstract words
    D. Use a passive tone

    4.____

5. Messages between departments in an agency are usually sent by:

    A. Letter
    B. Memo
    C. Telegram
    D. Long reports

    5.____

6. Repetitive work can be simplified by the use of:

    A. Memos
    B. Telegrams
    C. Forms
    D. Reports

    6.____

7. In filling out forms and applications, it is important to be:

    A. Legible
    B. Complete
    C. Accurate
    D. All of the above

    7.____

8. Memos should be:

   A. Clear
   B. Brief
   C. Complete
   D. All of the above

9. Minutes of meetings should not include:

   A. The opinions of the recorder
   B. The approval of previous minutes
   C. The corrections of previous minutes
   D. The voting members present

10. Reports are written by public service workers to:

    A. Assemble information in one place
    B. Aid the organization in making decisions
    C. Inform the public and other agencies
    D. All of the above

11. News releases should include:

    A. A lead paragraph summarizing the story
    B. Long paragraphs about many topics
    C. The writer's opinion
    D. All of the above

12. Readers of news releases and reports are influenced by the:

    A. Content of the material
    B. Accuracy of the material
    C. Physical appearance of the material
    D. All of the above

13. The contents of a report should include:

    A. A description of the problem
    B. The questions to be answered
    C. Unimportant information
    D. A summary of findings

14. People tend to be influenced easier if:

    A. They can see something in the position that would be advantageous to them
    B. They are almost ready to agree anyhow
    C. The appeal to the emotions is not overly strong
    D. All of the above

KEY (CORRECT ANSWERS)

1. B
2. A
3. B
4. A
5. B

6. C
7. D
8. D
9. A
10. D

11. A
12. D
13. C
14. D

PROOFREADING

TABLE OF CONTENTS

	Page
PROOFREADER'S MARKS	1
Insert Period ... Caps-Used in Margin	1
Parentheses ... Lower Case-Used in Margin	2
Use Ligature ... Caps S Small Caps-Used in Text	3
TYPOGRAPHICAL ERRORS	4

PROOFREADING

PROOFREADER'S MARKS

⊙	INSERT PERIOD	▢	INDENT 1 EM
⋀	INSERT COMMA	▭	INDENT 2 EMS
;	INSERT COLON	¶	PARAGRAPH
?	INSERT QUESTION MARK	no ¶	NO PARAGRAPH
!	INSERT EXCLAMATION MARK	tr	TRANSPOSE-USED IN MARGIN
=/	INSERT HYPHEN	∿	TRANSPOSE-USED IN TEXT
∨	INSERT APOSTROPHE	sp	SPELL OUT
∨ ∨	INSERT QUOTATION MARKS	ital	ITALIC-USED IN MARGIN
⊢	INSERT 1-EN DASH	———	ITALIC-USED IN TEXT
⊢	INSERT 1-EM DASH	b.f.	BOLDFACE-USED IN MARGIN
#	Insert Space	⁓⁓⁓	BOLDFACE-USED IN TEXT
ld>	INSERT LEAD	s.c.	SMALL CAPS-USED IN MARGIN
shill	INSERT VIRGULE	═	SMALL CAPS-USED IN TEXT
∨	SUPERIOR	rom.	ROMAN TYPE
∧	INFERIOR	Caps.	CAPS-USED IN MARGIN

(/) PARENTHESES   ≡   CAPS-USED IN TEXT

[/] BRACKETS   l.c. LOWER CASE-USED IN MARGIN

/   LOWER CASE-USED IN TEXT

w.f. LOWER CASE-USED IN TEXT

⌢   CLOSE UP

𝑓   DELETE

𝒯   CLOSE UP AND DELETE

∂   CORRECT THE POSITION

⌐   MOVE RIGHT

⌐   MOVE LEFT

⊓   MOVE UP

⊔   MOVE DOWN

|| ALIGN VERTICALLY

=   ALIGN HORIZONTALLY

⊐⊏   CENTER HORIZONTALLY

⊔⊓   CENTER VERTICALLY

⌣   PUSH DOWN SPACE

⌒ USE LIGATURE

eq.# EQUALIZE SPACE-USED IN MARGIN

√√√ EQUALIZE SPACE-USED IN TEXT

√ DECREASE SPACE

stet LET IT STAND-USED IN MARGIN

. . . . . . LET IT STAND-USED IN TEXT

⊗ DIRTY OR BROKEN LETTER

run over CARRY OVER TO NEXT LINE

run back CARRY BACK TO PRECEDING LINE

copy out SOMETHING OMITTED-SEE COPY

au? ? QUESTION TO AUTHOR

∧ CARET-GENERAL INDICATOR USED TO MARK EXACT POSITION OF ERROR IN TEXT

; INSERT SEMICOLON

C • sc CAPS & SMALL CAPS-USED IN MARGIN

≡ CAPS & SMALL CAPS-USED IN TEXT

TYPOGRAPHICAL ERRORS

It does not appear that the earliest printers had any method of correcting errors before the form was on the press. The learned The learned correctors of the first two centures of printing were not proofreaders in our sense; they were rather what we should term office editors. Their labors were chiefly to see that the proof corresponded to the copy, but that the printed page was correct in its Latinity; that the words were there, and that the sense was right. They cared but little about orthography, bad letters, or purely printers' errors, and when the text seemed to them wrong they consulted fresh authorities or altered it on their own responsibility. Good proofs, in the modern sense, were impossible until professional readers were employed, men who had first a printer's education, and then spent many years in the correction of proof. The orthography of English, which for the past century has undergone little change, was very fluctuating until after the publication of Johnson's Dictionary, and capitals, which have been used with considerable regularity for the past 80 years, were previously used on the miss for hit plan. The approach to regularity, so far as we have may be attributed to the growth of a class of professional proofreaders, and it is to them that we owe the correctness of modern printing. More errors have been found in the Bible than in any other one work. For many generations it was frequently the case that Bibles were brought out stealthily, from fear of governmental interference. They were frequently printed from imperfect texts, and were often modified to meet the views of those who published them. The story is related that a certain woman in Germany, who was the wife of a printer and who had become disgusted with the continual assertions of the superiority of man over woman which she had heard, hurried into the composing room while her husband was at supper and altered a sentence in the Bible, which he was printing, so that it read Narr instead of Herr, thus making the verse read "And he shall be thy fool" instead of "And he shall be thy lord." The word not was omitted by Barker, the King's printer in England in 1632, in printing the seventh commandment. He was fined £3,000 on this account.

www.ingramcontent.com/pod-product-compliance
Lightning Source LLC
Chambersburg PA
CBHW082039300426
44117CB00015B/2544